SHADOW ARMIES

The Secret Resistance Networks That Crippled Hitler's War Machine

CHUCK WATSON

Shadow Armies

The Secret Resistance Networks That Crippled Hitler's War Machine

Chuck Watson

Crazy Dog Publishing

Published by Crazy Dog Publishing LLC

ISBN (Paperback): 979-8-950354-00-7

ISBN (eBook): 979-8-950354-09-0

Cover imagery generated with AI assistance and designed by Chuck Watson

For the shadow fighters of France, Poland, and Yugoslavia — the farmers and teachers, the students and librarians, the ordinary people who chose an extraordinary path when darkness fell across their world. They carried no flags and wore no uniforms. They fought alone, in secret, and often died the same way. History remembers the generals. This book is for the rest.

TABLE OF CONTENTS

LONDON
BELGIUM
GERMANY
English Channel
Caen
PARIS
Strassbourg
Rennes
Seine
ITALY
Lyon
ATLANTIC
OCEAN
Loire
Alpes
Bordeaux
VICHY
Marseille
PYRÉNÉES
SPAIN
N
W   E
S
MEDITERRANEAN
SEA
50 KM   100 KM
0
0   50 MI   100 MI
FRANCE
1940—1944

The Baker Street Irregulars

How Britain Built a Secret Army Inside France

The order came down from the very top, and it was characteristically blunt. In the summer of 1940, with France fallen, Dunkirk a fresh wound, and the Nazi war machine occupying the better part of Western Europe, Winston Churchill summoned Hugh Dalton, his newly appointed Minister of Economic Warfare, and issued a directive that would change the nature of modern warfare forever. "And now," Churchill told him, "Set Europe ablaze."

It sounded simple. It was anything but.

What Churchill envisioned was something that had never been attempted on such a scale — a secret army operating behind enemy lines, not in uniform, not under any flag, invisible to the naked eye but devastating in effect. Saboteurs. Spies. Organizers. Men and women who would slip into occupied Europe, disappear into the civilian population, and quietly dismantle Hitler's war machine from within. They would blow bridges and burn fuel depots. They would corrupt railway lines and destroy communications. They would arm and train local resistance fighters, turning the occupied populations of Europe into a weapon the Nazis could neither see nor stop.

The organization created to fulfill Churchill's vision was called the Special Operations Executive — SOE. And in the beginning, there were little more than a handful of determined people working out of a requisitioned office building in central London, armed with enthusiasm, a mandate from the Prime Minister, and almost nothing else.

The headquarters of SOE was located at 64 Baker Street — a fact that gave rise to its affectionate nickname among those who knew of its existence: the Baker Street Irregulars, borrowed from the gang of street informants who assisted Sherlock Holmes in Arthur Conan Doyle's stories. The comparison was apt. SOE was unconventional, improvised, and operated at the fringes of what the established military and intelligence services considered proper or even acceptable. MI6 viewed it with barely concealed contempt. The regular army regarded it with suspicion. The Foreign Office worried constantly about the diplomatic consequences of its operations. SOE existed in a state of permanent bureaucratic warfare almost as intense as the actual war it was supposed to be fighting.

What saved it — what gave it shape and doctrine and eventual effectiveness — was a small number of exceptional individuals who understood from the outset that this new kind of warfare required an entirely new way of thinking.

Chief among them was Major General Colin Gubbins, a compact, intense Scotsman who had spent years studying irregular warfare and had come away convinced that it was not merely a useful supplement to conventional military operations but potentially a decisive force in its own right. Gubbins had fought in Ireland during the War of Independence, watched the IRA run rings around the British Army with a fraction of the resources, and drawn his conclusions. He had written two influential pamphlets — *The Art of Guerrilla Warfare* and *The Partisan Leader's Handbook* — that would become the intellectual foundation of everything SOE attempted. When Churchill gave the order to set Europe ablaze, Gubbins was already thinking about how to light the match.

Under his influence SOE developed a doctrine built around three principles: organization, communication, and supply. You could not simply parachute agents into occupied territory and hope for the best. You needed networks — circuits, in SOE terminology — each with a clear structure. An organizer to build and lead the local resistance. A courier to move messages and materials between cells, keeping the network compartmentalized so that the capture of one agent could not unravel the whole. A wireless operator to maintain contact with London. Each role was critical. Each role was lethal if discovered.

Within SOE, the section responsible for occupied France was known as F Section — the F standing simply for France. It was F Section that would become both SOE's greatest achievement and the source of its most devastating failures.

Running the administrative machinery of F Section and doing so with an intensity that left everyone around her simultaneously awed and exhausted, was Vera Atkins — a Romanian-born intelligence officer of extraordinary ability whose precise role within SOE has been the subject of historical debate. Officially she was an intelligence officer, secretary to F Section's head, Maurice Buckmaster. In practice she was the operational heart of the entire enterprise.

It was Vera Atkins who interviewed prospective agents, who assessed their suitability with a cool and penetrating eye, who briefed them before they left — sometimes in the small hours of the morning before a predawn flight — and who pressed into their hands their cover documents, their escape materials, their final instructions. It was Vera Atkins who memorized the personal details of every agent she sent into the field: their cover names, their real names, the names of their families, their mannerisms and habits and weaknesses. And it was Vera Atkins who kept meticulous track of what happened to them once they were gone, who noticed when a wireless operator's transmission style subtly changed, who felt the first cold premonition when a circuit went silent.

She sent agents to their deaths. She knew it, and she did it anyway, because she understood better than almost anyone what was at stake. After the war she spent years tracking down the fates of the agents who had not come home, attending war crimes trials, piecing together the final hours of men and women she had personally dispatched into the darkness. It was a form of devotion that defied easy description.

The mechanics of inserting an agent into occupied France were themselves a small miracle of planning and improvisation.

Candidates for SOE service were recruited from a wide range of sources — men and women with French connections, language skills, knowledge of specific regions. They were approached discreetly, sometimes through personal contacts, sometimes through military channels, and their suitability assessed over a series of increasingly demanding tests. Many were rejected. Those who made it through faced a training program that had been built from scratch and refined through painful experience.

The early phases took place in country houses requisitioned across England — grand, drafty establishments given over to the unglamorous business of teaching people how to kill quietly, move invisibly, and survive interrogation. Students learned wireless operation, coded communications, the use of explosives, and the fundamentals of hand-to-hand combat. They were taught to pick locks, to follow and detect surveillance, to construct cover stories robust enough to withstand determined questioning. They were subjected to mock interrogations — sometimes brutal ones — to test their resistance under pressure.

Those who survived this phase moved on to the final and most demanding stage: paramilitary training in the Scottish Highlands, where agents parachuted from aircraft for the first time, learned to handle weapons in field conditions, and conducted exercises in the unforgiving terrain of the mountains. It was here that the reality of what they had volunteered for became impossible to ignore.

Then came the flight.

Agents were typically inserted into France in one of two ways. The first was by parachute, dropped from converted RAF Lysander or Halifax aircraft flying at low altitude through the night, guided to their landing zones by reception committees on the ground who signaled with torches in pre-arranged patterns. The second was by Lysander landing — a brief, extraordinarily delicate operation in which the small aircraft touched down in a dark field for no more than a few minutes, exchanging outgoing agents for incoming ones before taking off again into the night. Both methods required precise coordination, favorable weather, and more than a little luck.

What awaited agents on the ground was a France divided and dangerous in ways that London could only partially understand.

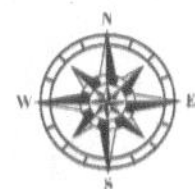

The early history of SOE's F Section in France was, by any honest accounting, a story of catastrophic failure as much as heroic endeavor.

The first circuits established in occupied France were blown with shocking speed. Agents who had seemed promising in training made elementary errors in the field — mistakes born of inexperience, overconfidence, or simply the impossible difficulty of maintaining a false identity under constant pressure. Cover stories that had seemed airtight in London unraveled in the face of routine German security checks. Networks that had taken months to build collapsed in days when a single agent was captured and, under torture, gave up what they knew.

The Germans were formidable opponents. The Gestapo and the Abwehr — Germany's military intelligence service — were experienced, well-resourced, and thoroughly embedded in the French civilian administration. The collaborationist Vichy government provided them with access to French police records and administrative databases that made the maintenance of false identities exponentially more difficult. Informers were everywhere, motivated by ideology, fear, personal grudges, or simple greed. The occupied zone of northern France was a surveillance state of considerable efficiency.

SOE's wireless communications were vulnerable in ways that took time to fully appreciate. The Germans operated mobile direction-finding vans that could triangulate the position of a transmitting wireless set within minutes. Operators were instructed to keep transmissions short and to change locations frequently, but in practice the pressure of operational necessity often kept them on the air longer than was safe. Several early operators were captured at their sets.

There was also the grim phenomenon SOE came to call the "playback" — the practice by which German intelligence, having captured a wireless operator, would force or persuade them to continue transmitting to London under German control, feeding false information and luring additional agents and supply drops into compromised territory. The detection of a playback required London to notice subtle anomalies in transmission style or content — a task that fell, in large part, to Vera Atkins and her colleagues, and one at which they did not always succeed.

But SOE learned. Painfully, at great human cost, it learned.

Security protocols were tightened. Circuits were restructured to minimize the damage that any single capture could cause. Training was improved, cover stories made more sophisticated, wireless procedures made more stringent. A dedicated forgery operation — one of the unsung masterpieces of the entire war — produced identity documents of such quality that they became virtually indistinguishable from the genuine article. Craftsmen who had worked in printing and engraving before the war now turned their skills to producing identity passes, ration cards, work permits, and travel documents without which movement in occupied France was impossible.

New agents — better trained, better prepared, more carefully selected — began to arrive in France through 1942 and into 1943. Among them were individuals of extraordinary caliber: men and women who would build circuits that survived, that grew, that eventually became the foundation of a genuine shadow army capable of striking at the heart of the Nazi occupation.

Churchill had wanted Europe set ablaze. His Baker Street Irregulars were learning, slowly and at terrible cost, how to hold the match.

The fire, when it finally came, would change everything.

The White Mouse

Nancy Wake and the Art of Invisible War

She was not what the Gestapo expected. That was, in the end, the whole point.

Nancy Wake arrived in France in the 1930s as a young Australian journalist with a press credential, a sharp eye, and an appetite for life that the narrow world she had grown up in simply could not contain. Born in Wellington, New Zealand in 1912 and raised in Australia, she had scraped together enough money to buy a one-way ticket out of Sydney at the age of sixteen and never looked back. By the time she settled in Marseille and married Henri Fiocca — a wealthy French industrialist who adored her completely — she had already seen enough of Europe to understand what was coming. She had watched Hitler's rallies from the crowd in Vienna in the early 1930s, seen the faces of the men cheering, and felt something cold move through her that she would not forget.

When France fell in June 1940 and the German occupation began, Nancy Wake made a decision that would cost her everything she had built — her marriage, her home, her safety, her life as she knew it — and she made it without apparent hesitation. She would fight.

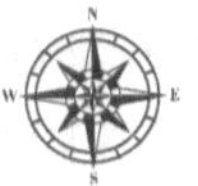

The Pat O'Leary Line was one of the most important escape networks operating across both zones of occupied France — moving Allied airmen and fugitives southward through German-controlled territory and the collaborationist Vichy zone toward the Spanish border— a clandestine organization that moved Allied airmen, escaped prisoners of war, and others at risk of capture southward through France and over the Pyrenees into neutral Spain. It was dangerous, exhausting, and absolutely vital work. Nancy Wake threw herself into it.

Using her social position, her fluency in French, her natural confidence, and the cover provided by her husband's business connections, she became one of the network's most effective couriers. She carried messages, forged documents, and at times the airmen themselves — walking them through checkpoints with a brazenness that left her colleagues simultaneously breathless and terrified. She was, by multiple accounts, extraordinarily good at it. She had the actor's gift of complete conviction, the ability to inhabit a role so thoroughly that the performance became indistinguishable from reality.

The Gestapo noticed. They always noticed, eventually. By 1943 they had identified an elusive female operative working in the Marseille region and given her a nickname that she would carry for the rest of her life: *die Weiße Maus* — the White Mouse. The name captured something essential about her. She was always there and never there, slipping through their fingers every time they reached for her.

By late 1943 the net was closing. Henri Fiocca, who had supported and protected his wife's activities throughout, urged her to run. The Germans were watching their house. Arrest was a matter of days, perhaps hours. Nancy Wake crossed the Pyrenees on foot in the dead of winter, was captured by Spanish border guards, talked her way out of detention, and eventually made her way to Britain.

She left Henri behind. She would not see him again. The Germans arrested him shortly after her escape and, unable to find her, tortured and executed him in 1943. He had refused to tell them anything. Nancy Wake learned of his death only after the war ended.

In Britain, the SOE found in Nancy Wake something rare — an agent with real operational experience in occupied France, genuine language fluency, an established understanding of how the resistance functioned on the ground, and a personal motivation that needed no augmenting. She was assessed, recruited, and put through the full SOE training program.

She was, by her own later account and the accounts of her instructors, an exceptional student — not because she was naturally gifted at every skill but because she approached each one with a ferocity that left little room for failure. Parachute training at Ringway near Manchester. Weapons handling and fieldcraft in the Scottish Highlands. Explosives. Unarmed combat. The full curriculum that SOE put every agent through, and many did not survive in the purely psychological sense — the training revealed, with brutal clarity, exactly what you were being prepared to do and what would happen if you were caught.

Her unarmed combat instructor, a former Shanghai policeman named William Fairbairn who had spent decades developing practical killing techniques, later described her as one of the most determined students he had trained. The skills he taught were not sport. They were designed for one purpose: to kill another human being quickly and quietly before they could raise an alarm. Nancy Wake learned them and did not flinch.

On the night of February 29, 1944, she parachuted back into France — tangled her parachute in a tree on landing, was helped down by a reception committee member who remarked that he hoped all trees in France bore such beautiful fruit, and reportedly told him that she hoped all Frenchmen were not as fresh as he was. It was, in its way, a perfect Nancy Wake entrance.

What she found in the Auvergne — the rugged volcanic plateau in south-central France where she was assigned to work — was a Maquis force of considerable size and almost no discipline. The Maquis were the rural resistance fighters of France, young men who had fled to the hills and forests rather than submit to the forced labor programs the German occupation authorities were imposing on the French population. They were brave, motivated, and in many cases dangerously disorganized.

Nancy Wake was assigned as liaison between the Maquis and London — responsible for coordinating supply drops, communicating the group's needs and activities to SOE headquarters, and helping to shape the fighters into something that could function as an effective military force. She was, in practice, far more than a liaison. She became a commander.

At its peak the Maquis force she worked with in the Auvergne numbered approximately 7,000 fighters. She organized them, disciplined them, cajoled and occasionally berated them into operating with the kind of security and coordination that kept them alive. She participated in arms drops, led raids on German installations, and planned operations against the infrastructure the Germans needed to move troops and supplies through central France. The sabotage campaign she helped coordinate contributed directly to the disruption of German military movement ahead of the Allied landings in southern France in August 1944.

She also killed men. This is documented and she never denied it. In her later memoirs and interviews she spoke about it with a directness that made some audience members uncomfortable. She had done what the war required. She was not sorry.

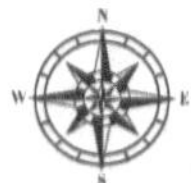

The bicycle journey has become the most famous single episode of Nancy Wake's war, and it deserves its fame — though it is worth being precise about what is documented and what has accumulated in the retelling.

The situation was this: her wireless operator, a man named Denis Rake, had been forced to flee the Maquis camp in a hurry during a German sweep of the area, and in the chaos the codes needed to communicate with London had been lost or destroyed. Without the codes, the wireless set was useless. Without the wireless set, there was no communication with London, no ability to call in supply drops, no operational link to SOE headquarters.

Nancy Wake got on a bicycle and rode to find another circuit that could provide replacement codes. The journey covered approximately 500 kilometers — roughly 310 miles — through countryside that was thick with German checkpoints and patrol activity. She completed it in just over seventy hours, passing through multiple checkpoints using her cover identity and her nerve.

When she returned to camp, she was so exhausted she could barely stand. She reportedly wept — not from fear or grief but from pure physical depletion, the body finally surrendering after the will had kept it moving long past its limits. Then she slept, and when she woke, she went back to work.

The killing of the SS sentry is the episode that separates the documented record from the more contested terrain of memoir and legend, and it requires careful handling.

Nancy Wake stated in her 1985 autobiography and in subsequent interviews that on one occasion, when a German sentry discovered the Maquis camp and she was the closest person to him, she killed him with her bare hands — a technique learned from her SOE unarmed combat training — to prevent him from raising an alarm. She described the act with characteristic bluntness: she had used a specific hold, broken his neck, and felt nothing about it except relief that the camp had been protected.

This account has not been independently corroborated by other sources, and some historians treat it with caution given that it rests entirely on Wake's own testimony. It is included here because she was a credible witness to her own life, because her account was consistent across multiple tellings, and because the technique she described was precisely what SOE unarmed combat training taught. It is presented as her account, not as verified fact.

What is not in dispute is that Nancy Wake was entirely capable of it.

The war ended and she came home to discover that home no longer existed.

Henri was dead. The house in Marseille was gone. The social world she had inhabited — the dinner parties, the easy wealth, the life of a prosperous French industrialist's wife — had been consumed by the same fire she had helped to light. She received decorations from three governments: the George Medal from Britain, the Médaille de la Résistance from France, and the Medal of Freedom from the United States. She was, by any measure, one of the most decorated servicewomen of the Second World War.

It was not enough. It could not be enough. The cost of what she had chosen was not measured in medals.

She spent the rest of a very long life — she died in London in 2011 at the age of ninety-eight — carrying what she had seen and done with the same directness she had brought to everything else. She did not romanticize it. She did not regret it. She had made her choices with open eyes, paid the price they demanded, and refused to pretend that the price had been small.

The White Mouse had run her last race. It had lasted thirty years, covered more ground than most people travel in a lifetime, and left a mark on the war in France that no amount of time has managed to erase.

Seventeen Days to Normandy

How the Resistance Stopped an SS Panzer Division

On the night of June 5, 1944, the BBC French Service broadcast something that sounded, to any casual listener, like pure nonsense. Buried within the regular evening transmission, between news bulletins and music programming, came a string of seemingly random phrases — fragments of poetry, lines from songs, disconnected images that meant nothing to anyone who did not know what to listen for. But across occupied France, in farmhouses and barns and back rooms and cellars, men and women bent over hidden radio sets and listened with absolute attention. They had been waiting months for these words.

Among the phrases broadcast that night were the opening lines of a poem by Paul Verlaine — *Les sanglots longs des violons de l'automne* — the long sobs of autumn's violins. It was the signal. The Allied invasion of France was imminent. The time for preparation was over. The time to act had come.

What followed over the next several weeks was one of the most extraordinary sabotage campaigns in the history of warfare — and one of the most consequential. The French Resistance, coordinated by SOE's F Section and armed with detailed operational plans that had been months in preparation, rose up across the length and breadth of occupied France and began systematically destroying everything the German military needed to move troops and supplies to the Normandy front. Railways. Bridges. Fuel depots. Telephone lines. The infrastructure of occupation, built and maintained at enormous cost, began coming apart at the seams.

Nowhere was the impact of this campaign more dramatically demonstrated than in the story of the 2nd SS Panzer Division — Das Reich — and its seventeen-day journey from Toulouse to Normandy.

Das Reich was one of the most formidable, armored divisions in the German order of battle — a veteran formation that had fought on the Eastern Front, equipped with Panzer IV tanks and the fearsome Panther, and staffed by experienced, battle-hardened soldiers. In early June 1944 it was resting and refitting near Toulouse in southern France, far from the front, its commanders expecting a period of relative quiet before whatever the Allies had planned next revealed itself.

The Allied landings at Normandy on June 6 changed everything. Das Reich received orders to move north immediately and join the defense of the Normandy bridgehead. The journey from Toulouse to the Norman front was approximately 450 miles. Under normal conditions, moving a mechanized division along the roads and railways of France, the journey should have taken no more than three days — perhaps less.

It took seventeen.

The delay was not an accident. It was not bad luck or poor planning on the German side. It was the result of a deliberate, coordinated, and ferociously executed sabotage campaign that had been planned in London, prepared in the field over many months, and unleashed the moment the BBC broadcast its coded signals into the French night.

The operational blueprint for the railway sabotage campaign was known as Plan Vert — Green Plan — one of a series of color-coded sabotage schemes developed by SOE in coordination with the French resistance organization and the Allied high command in the months before D-Day. Plan Vert was specifically designed to destroy the French railway network in a way that would prevent the Germans from using it to reinforce Normandy. It was extraordinarily detailed — identifying specific targets, prioritizing cuts that would cause maximum disruption, and assigning responsibility for each target to specific resistance circuits.

The BBC broadcast activated it.

Within hours of the signal, resistance teams across southern and central France were in motion. Railway sabotage was their primary task, and they approached it with the thoroughness of people who had been preparing for exactly this moment for a very long time. The methods were varied and effective. Rail lines were cut at carefully chosen points — not merely broken but destroyed, sections of track removed or twisted beyond quick repair. Locomotives were sabotaged in their sheds, their mechanical components destroyed or stolen, rendering them useless without the specialized parts that could take days or weeks to source and install. Signaling equipment was wrecked. Railway bridges were demolished where the resistance had the explosives and the time to do it properly.

The SOE agents who had spent the previous months building and arming the circuits that carried out these attacks now became coordinators and advisors — working alongside French resistance leaders to identify the highest-priority targets, ensure that explosives were used effectively, and communicate results back to London. Among them was a network of Jedburgh teams — the three-man Allied special forces units parachuted into France specifically to work with the resistance — who brought military expertise and direct radio links to Allied command.

The telephone and telegraph network was attacked simultaneously. Lines were cut, exchanges sabotaged, the communication infrastructure that the German military depended on to coordinate its movements reduced to a patchwork of gaps and silences. German commanders found themselves unable to communicate reliably with their superiors or with each other, forced to dispatch motorcycle couriers along roads that were themselves under attack.

The road network was the third axis of the campaign. Bridges were blown. Fuel depots — critical for a motorized division that consumed enormous quantities of petrol simply to move — were attacked and destroyed. Ambushes were laid on the roads Das Reich needed to use, harassing the column, forcing it to halt, compelling it to deploy infantry to clear resistance fighters who melted back into the countryside before they could be caught and destroyed.

For the men of Das Reich, the journey north became a slow nightmare of frustration and fury. The division moved in fits and starts, halted repeatedly by demolished bridges, destroyed rail infrastructure, ambushes from fighters who disappeared into the bocage and the forests before they could be engaged effectively. Detours added miles and hours. Fuel shortages — the result of the attacks on supply depots — forced the column to wait while resupply was organized. Mechanical breakdowns that might have been quickly repaired became major delays when the parts needed were unavailable.

The commanders of Das Reich were experienced soldiers who understood, with increasing and enraging clarity, exactly what was happening to them. They were being systematically delayed by an invisible enemy — an enemy that struck and vanished, that could not be brought to battle and destroyed in the conventional sense, that seemed to be everywhere and nowhere simultaneously.

Their response to this impotence was catastrophic.

The town of Tulle sits in the Corrèze valley in south-central France, a modest provincial town of no particular military significance. On June 7, 1944 — the day after D-Day — resistance fighters of the local Maquis briefly captured the town from its German garrison, killing a number of soldiers in the fighting.

When Das Reich's advance units arrived the following day and retook Tulle, the reprisal was swift and savage. The divisional commander ordered that a significant number of the town's male population be hanged as a collective punishment for the resistance action. Ninety-nine men were selected — many of them with no connection to the Maquis — and hanged from the lampposts and balconies along the main street of the town, their bodies left on display as a warning.

Dozens more were deported to concentration camps, most of whom did not survive the war.

The massacre at Tulle was horrific. What happened two days later at Oradour-sur-Glane was worse.

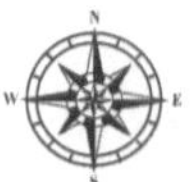

Oradour-sur-Glane was a small village in the Haute-Vienne department — a quiet, unremarkable place of perhaps 650 inhabitants. On the afternoon of June 10, 1944, troops from the Der Führer regiment of Das Reich entered the village, ordered the entire population to assemble in the market square, and then systematically murdered them all.

The men of the village were separated into groups and taken to barns and outbuildings, where they were shot. The women and children — including infants — were herded into the village church. The church was set on fire. Those who attempted to escape the flames were shot. When it was over, 642 people were dead. The village was burned to the ground.

The reasons for the specific choice of Oradour-sur-Glane remain historically contested. Some accounts suggest the troops were looking for a different village — Oradour-sur-Vayres, some distance away — where a German officer had allegedly been taken prisoner by the Maquis. Others suggest it was a deliberate act of terror, chosen at random to maximize psychological impact on the surrounding population. What is not contested is what happened, or who did it. The perpetrators were identified. A trial was eventually held, decades later, though justice — in any meaningful sense — proved as elusive as the resistance fighters the division had never managed to catch.

The ruins of Oradour-sur-Glane were left standing by order of the French government after the war — preserved exactly as Das Reich left them, a permanent memorial to what had been done there. They stand to this day.

Das Reich finally reached the Normandy front on June 23, 1944 — seventeen days after receiving its orders to move. By the time it arrived, the Allied beachhead had been consolidated, reinforced, and made essentially impregnable. The window in which an armored counterattack by a fresh, veteran division might have pushed the Allies back into the sea had closed.

The precise strategic weight of the delay is a matter historians continue to debate, and it is important to be honest about the limits of what can be definitively claimed. The Normandy campaign was shaped by many factors — Allied air superiority, German command failures, the success of Operation Fortitude in keeping Hitler convinced that the main invasion was still coming at Pas-de-Calais. The seventeen-day delay of Das Reich was one thread in a very complex tapestry.

But it was not an insignificant thread. The Allied commanders who had planned the resistance sabotage campaign understood its purpose — to deny the Germans the ability to concentrate their armored forces against the beachhead in the critical first days after the landings, when the Allied position was most vulnerable. By that measure, the campaign succeeded. Das Reich arrived too late to matter.

The men and women of the French Resistance who demolished the railways and blew the bridges and ambushed the columns had done what they set out to do. They had bought time with their courage — and, in ways they had not chosen and could not control, with the lives of the innocent people of Tulle and Oradour-sur-Glane.

That is the unbearable arithmetic of resistance warfare, and there is no way to make it balance.

The Prosper Disaster

Betrayal in the Heart of France

In the spring of 1943, the Prosper network was the crown jewel of SOE's F Section operations in occupied France. It stretched across northern France like a web — hundreds of agents, sub-circuits, weapons caches, and safe houses, all connected to a central organization of remarkable sophistication and reach. It had taken nearly two years to build. It collapsed in a matter of weeks.

The story of what happened to Prosper — and why — is one of the most debated and disturbing episodes in the entire history of the Special Operations Executive. It is a story of courage, of catastrophic failure, and of a mystery at its center that has never been fully resolved. Depending on which theory you find most persuasive, it is either a tale of operational misfortune and German cunning, or something considerably darker — a deliberate sacrifice of human lives in the service of a strategic deception. The evidence supports elements of both interpretations. Neither fully satisfies. The truth, to the extent it can be recovered at all, lies somewhere in the wreckage.

Francis Suttill was not a romantic figure in the conventional sense. He was a lawyer — precise, methodical, deeply serious — a Franco-British barrister of thirty-two who had been recruited by SOE in 1942 and sent to France in October of that year with the code name PROSPER, which became the name of the circuit he built. He was not given to the kind of dashing improvisation that characterized some SOE agents. His strength was organizational — the patient, painstaking construction of a network that could survive the inevitable pressures of operating in occupied territory.

And build he did. By early 1943 the Prosper circuit had become the largest SOE network in France. Its geographic reach extended across the Île-de-France, the Loire Valley, and into Normandy and the north. It encompassed dozens of sub-circuits, each with its own organizer, courier, and wireless operator. It maintained hundreds of weapons caches — rifles, Sten guns, explosives, ammunition — carefully hidden across the region for the day when the Allies would land and the resistance would rise. It had safe houses in Paris and across the countryside, a network of couriers who moved messages and materials with practiced efficiency, and contacts within the French population at virtually every level of society.

Suttill ran it with meticulous care. He understood the importance of compartmentalization — keeping different parts of the network separate so that the capture of one agent could not unravel the whole. He understood the danger of careless talk, of meetings in exposed locations, of wireless operators who stayed on the air too long. He understood all of it, and he tried to build accordingly.

It was not enough.

The unraveling began in the early summer of 1943, and when it came it was shockingly swift.

The first arrests happened in late June. A handful of agents — peripheral figures in the network — were picked up by the Gestapo in what initially appeared to be routine security sweeps. Then more arrests followed, in rapid succession, moving inward through the circuit like a hand closing into a fist. Sub-circuit after sub-circuit went dark. Safe houses were raided. Weapons caches were found and seized. Couriers were picked up on the roads between Paris and the Loire.

On June 24, 1943, Francis Suttill himself was arrested in Paris. His second-in-command, Gilbert Norman — the circuit's wireless operator, code name ARCHAMBAUD — had been arrested days earlier. Andrée Borrel, one of the circuit's most capable couriers and a woman of extraordinary courage who had been among the first female agents SOE sent to France, was arrested around the same time.

Within weeks, the Prosper network — two years in the building, hundreds of agents strong, the most ambitious SOE operation in occupied France — had ceased to exist. Estimates of the total number of arrests vary, but historians generally place the figure at somewhere between four hundred and five hundred people — agents, resistance contacts, and French civilians who had provided shelter or assistance.

The scale of the collapse was almost incomprehensible. How had it happened?

The simplest and most widely accepted explanation centers on a series of security failures that, taken together, created the conditions for catastrophic penetration by German intelligence.

The Prosper circuit had grown very large, very fast — and size was the enemy of security. The principle of compartmentalization that Suttill understood in theory had proved difficult to maintain in practice as the network expanded. Too many people knew too much. Too many connections existed between different parts of the circuit. When the Germans pulled on one thread, they found it connected to dozens of others.

There is also strong evidence that the circuit had been penetrated by at least one double agent. The most likely candidate, identified by multiple historians, was a man named Henri Déricourt — an SOE air movements officer responsible for organizing Lysander landing operations in the field. Déricourt is now believed, based on postwar evidence including his own admissions, to have been working for the German SD — the intelligence branch of the SS — while simultaneously working for SOE. He provided the Germans with copies of mail carried on the Lysander flights, giving them detailed intelligence about agents, circuits, and operations. Whether his penetration directly triggered the Prosper collapse or was one of several contributing factors remains debated, but the consensus among historians is that he was a genuine and damaging agent of German intelligence operating at the heart of SOE's French operations.

A third factor was the behavior of Gilbert Norman after his arrest. There is credible evidence — though its precise extent is disputed — that Norman cooperated with his German captors to a degree that went beyond what could be attributed to torture alone. Some accounts suggest he provided the Gestapo with information about the circuit's structure and personnel. This remains one of the most sensitive and contested aspects of the entire affair, not least because Norman died in Mauthausen concentration camp in September 1944 and could not speak for himself after the war.

These three factors — the circuit's unwieldy size, Déricourt's betrayal, and the possible compromise of Norman — would, in combination, go a long way toward explaining how Prosper collapsed so completely and so quickly. For many historians they are sufficient explanation. But there is a fourth theory, and it is considerably more troubling.

The controversial suggestion — first raised seriously in the 1950s and pursued with particular tenacity by the historian Francis Foot and later by Jean Overton Fuller and others — is that the collapse of the Prosper network was not entirely accidental. That SOE leadership, or elements of the British intelligence community above SOE, may have deliberately allowed the circuit to be compromised as part of a broader strategic deception operation designed to convince Hitler that the Allied invasion of France would come not at Normandy but somewhere else.

The argument runs as follows. In 1943 the Allied high command was deep in the planning of Operation Overlord — the Normandy landings — and was acutely aware that its success depended on keeping the Germans uncertain about where the blow would fall. One component of the deception strategy involved convincing the Germans that an Allied landing in the Pas-de-Calais or somewhere in northern France was imminent in 1943 — a feint that would tie down German forces and complicate their defensive planning.

Some accounts suggest that Suttill was given hints — deliberately misleading ones — that an Allied landing in France was coming in 1943, and that he passed this information to his network. The suggestion is that this was done intentionally, to make the Prosper circuit behave in ways consistent with preparations for an imminent invasion, thereby feeding the German intelligence services a picture that served Allied deception goals — even if doing so meant making the circuit more visible and more vulnerable.

Whatever its causes, the human consequences of the Prosper disaster were devastating and irreversible.

Of the agents arrested in the collapse, the majority did not survive the war. They were held in French prisons — Fresnes, in Paris, was the most common initial destination — interrogated by the Gestapo and eventually transported to concentration camps in Germany. SOE's female agents were covered by the protections of the Geneva Convention to an even lesser degree than their male counterparts, and the Germans treated them accordingly.

Andrée Borrel — the courier who had been one of the first women SOE sent to France, a woman who had helped build the Prosper network from its earliest days — was transported to Natzweiler-Struthof concentration camp in Alsace and killed there in July 1944, injected with phenol and then cremated while still alive according to survivor testimony. She was twenty-nine years old.

Francis Suttill was taken to Germany and executed at Sachsenhausen concentration camp in March 1945 — weeks before the camp was liberated by Allied forces. He had been held for almost two years.

Gilbert Norman died at Mauthausen in September 1944.

Dozens of French civilians who had sheltered agents, hidden weapons, or passed messages — people who had made the choice to help and had asked for nothing in return — were arrested, tortured, and deported. Many of them died in the camps. They are the least visible casualties of the Prosper disaster, the ones whose names appear in no operational histories and whose courage will never be fully documented.

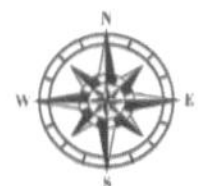

The Prosper disaster shook SOE to its foundations. It forced a reckoning with the vulnerabilities that had been allowed to develop — the overextended networks, the compromised security procedures, the dangers of trusting the wrong people in an environment where the wrong people were everywhere.

It also forced, in time, a confrontation with the question that the controversial theory raises and that no amount of historical investigation has yet been able to fully lay to rest: whether the men and women of the Prosper circuit were betrayed not only by German intelligence and by the accidents of operational security, but by the very organization that had sent them into the field.

No definitive answer has emerged. The classified files that might settle the question — if such files exist and if they say what the theory's proponents believe they say — have not been released in any form that resolves the debate. What remains is the documented record of what the circuit achieved, what it suffered, and what was lost when it fell.

Hundreds of people were arrested. Dozens executed. A two-year effort was destroyed in weeks.

And at the center of it all, a question that the history of the Second World War has never fully answered: who, in the end, was responsible for what happened to Prosper?

Jedburgh

The Men Who Dropped Blind

The briefing was thorough. The maps were detailed. The intelligence was as complete as London could have made it. And then the door of the aircraft opened at a thousand feet over occupied France in the middle of the night, and everything the briefing had prepared you for dissolved into the darkness rushing up from below, and you jumped anyway.

This was the essential experience of the Jedburgh teams — three men, parachuting blind into hostile territory, carrying a radio set, a weapons cache, and orders that assumed a level of local knowledge and operational stability that frequently bore no resemblance to what they found on the ground. They were soldiers, not spies. They wore uniform — deliberately, so that if captured they could claim the protections of the Geneva Convention, however unreliably those protections were honored by the Germans who caught them. They were supposed to link up with local Maquis commanders, assess the resistance forces in their area, call in supply drops, and coordinate sabotage operations in support of the Allied campaign. The theory was clean. The practice was something else entirely.

Between June and September 1944, ninety-three Jedburgh teams were inserted into occupied France. They operated in conditions of almost constant improvisation, chronic supply shortages, and relentless German pressure. Some were captured within days of landing. Others fought for months, coordinating operations that tied down German forces across the length and breadth of France. All of them discovered, with varying degrees of shock, that the gap between the planning room in London and the reality of the French countryside was wider than any briefing could have prepared them for.

The concept behind the Jedburgh program was developed jointly by SOE and the American Office of Strategic Services — the OSS, the wartime forerunner of the CIA — in 1943, as Allied planners began seriously working through the problem of how to maximize the contribution of the French resistance to the Normandy invasion. SOE's existing circuits were valuable, but they were primarily organized around the classic three-person cell structure — organizer, courier, wireless operator — optimized for clandestine intelligence work and small-scale sabotage. What the invasion would require was something more: the ability to rapidly organize, arm, and direct large bodies of resistance fighters in coordinated military operations across a wide geographic area, simultaneously with the conventional fighting on the beaches and in the bocage.

The solution was the Jedburgh team — a three-man unit composed of one American OSS officer, one British SOE officer, and one French officer from the Bureau Central de Renseignements et d'Action, the Free French intelligence and special operations organization. Each team carried a wireless set capable of communicating with the Allied Special Forces Headquarters in London, a personal weapons load, and enough supplies for initial operations. Their job was to be the bridge between the Allied high command and the French resistance on the ground — to speak both languages, military and resistance, and to translate between them under fire.

Recruitment was drawn from the special forces and intelligence communities of all three Allied nations. Candidates were assessed for language ability, physical fitness, psychological stability, and the kind of adaptability that irregular warfare demanded — the ability to function effectively when the plan had disintegrated and the only guide was judgment. Many applicants were rejected. Those who made it through faced a training program at Milton Hall, a requisitioned country house in Cambridgeshire, where Americans, British, and French officers trained together in conditions designed to build the kind of mutual confidence that would keep a three-man team functioning under extreme pressure.

It did not always work. The national tensions within Jedburgh teams were real and sometimes serious. American officers, trained in the direct culture of the US Army, sometimes chafed at the more indirect approach favored by their British counterparts. French officers — many of whom had spent years in exile watching their country occupied and their compatriots suffer — brought an intensity of personal motivation that their allies respected but did not always fully understand. The wireless operators, who were technically the junior members of each team, but whose skills were the team's lifeline to the outside world, occupied a peculiar position — indispensable and frequently overlooked.

What bound the teams together, in the end, was the shared experience of the jump.

Team Frederick dropped into the Breton countryside on the night of June 9, 1944 — three days after D-Day — becoming one of the first Jedburgh teams inserted into France. Its members were Major Adrian Wise of the British army, Lieutenant Paul Valentini of the French army, and Sergeant Louis Lajeunesse, the wireless operator. Their mission was to organize and arm the Maquis forces of Brittany in preparation for a potential Allied breakout through the region.

What they found on landing was organized chaos. The Breton resistance was large — estimates placed the total number of Maquis fighters in Brittany at somewhere between 30,000 and 35,000 — but it was poorly armed, inconsistently led, and operating under acute German pressure. The German garrison in Brittany was substantial and aggressive, conducting regular sweeps against known and suspected resistance concentrations.

Wise and his team spent their first weeks in constant motion, moving between Maquis groups, assessing their strength and organization, and transmitting requests for supply drops to London. The supply drops were the team's most critical function and its most persistent frustration. Drops required favorable weather, available aircraft, and the organization of reception committees on the ground — a coordination problem of considerable complexity when the parties involved were scattered across a large area, communicating by courier and subject to German interdiction at every point.

When the drops came through, they were transformative. A single successful supply drop could arm hundreds of fighters with rifles, Sten guns, plastic explosives, and ammunition — converting a poorly equipped band of determined civilians into something capable of genuine military action. Team Frederick coordinated dozens of such drops over the course of its operations, and the sabotage campaign that resulted — rail lines cut, bridges demolished, German communications disrupted — contributed directly to the difficulties the

German garrison experienced when the American break-out from Normandy swept into Brittany in late July 1944.

Team Hamish had a harder introduction to occupied France.

Dropping into the Nièvre department in central France on the night of June 6, 1944 — D-Day itself — the team consisted of Major John Smallwood of the British army, Captain Phillipe Ragueneau of the French army, and Sergeant Aubin Trettarre as wireless operator. Their landing went wrong from the moment they left the aircraft. Scattered by wind, the team members came down miles apart in unfamiliar countryside, with no reception committee and no immediate means of locating each other.

Smallwood spent the first hours after his landing moving cautiously through the darkness, hiding from German patrols that seemed to be everywhere, trying to establish where he was and whether his teammates had survived the drop. It took the better part of two days for the team to reassemble — two days during which each member was operating alone in hostile territory with limited supplies, no radio contact, and no way of knowing whether the others were alive or in German hands.

When they finally linked up and made contact with the local Maquis, they found a force of several thousand fighters — enthusiastic, motivated, and dangerously short of weapons and experienced leadership. The Maquis commanders were not always receptive to outside direction. They had been fighting and surviving in the Nièvre for months and years, developing their own methods and their own chains of command, and the arrival of three foreign officers with a radio set did not automatically confer authority.

The negotiation of that authority — establishing trust with local commanders, demonstrating genuine military competence, earning rather than demanding the cooperation of fighters who had no reason to defer to strangers — was one of the most consistently underestimated challenges the Jedburgh teams faced. The training at Milton Hall had prepared them for many things. The politics of working with proud, battle-hardened resistance leaders who had their own ideas about how the war should be fought in their own backyard had been harder to simulate.

Team Hamish worked through it. Smallwood's approach — patient, direct, willing to listen before acting — built the kind of working relationship with Maquis commanders that made coordinated operations possible. Over the following weeks the team called in supply drops that armed thousands of fighters, coordinated attacks on rail lines serving German forces moving toward Normandy, and organized ambushes on road convoys that cost the Germans men and material they could not easily replace.

Team Bugatti operated in the Dordogne, a region of southwestern France where the Maquis presence was strong but German counter-resistance activity was intense and often brutal. The team — Captain John Haskell of the OSS, Lieutenant René Couture of the French army, and Sergeant Fred Brousse as wireless operator — dropped in late June 1944 and immediately found themselves operating in conditions that tested every skill their training had given them.

The Dordogne Maquis were fighting a war that had been going on long before the Jedburgh teams arrived, and the cost had been high. Reprisals against civilian populations had created a landscape of grief and fury that gave the resistance its motivation and its ruthlessness in equal measure. The fighters Haskell and his team found were not the idealized guerrillas of the briefing room — they were exhausted, traumatized, sometimes barely organized, and operating in an environment where German security forces were conducting aggressive sweeps that could and did overrun Maquis camps with little warning.

The communications challenges the team faced were relentless. The wireless set — the team's single most critical piece of equipment — required a power source, sufficient transmission time to complete a message, and the ability to change locations frequently enough to avoid the German direction-finding vans that were always somewhere in the area. The operator, Brousse, became expert at the calculus of wireless work in the field — transmitting in short bursts, moving constantly, reading the landscape for high ground that improved signal quality and cover that reduced visibility.

The supply drops Team Bugatti coordinated armed thousands of Dordogne fighters and fueled a sabotage campaign that struck the railway lines, road bridges, and fuel installations the Germans needed to maintain their position in southwestern France. When Allied forces swept through the region in August 1944 they found a German garrison that had been systematically weakened, harassed, and deprived of the logistical support it needed to mount an effective defense.

The German response to Jedburgh operations was ferocious and consistent. Hitler had issued his Commando Order in October 1942, directing that Allied special forces operatives captured behind German lines were to be executed rather than treated as prisoners of war — regardless of whether they were in uniform. The order was a war crime under any legal standard, and it was not universally enforced, but it was enforced often enough to ensure that capture for a Jedburgh team member meant a very high probability of death.

Several Jedburgh teams were captured during the course of operations in France. Some team members were executed in accordance with the Commando Order. Others were sent to concentration camps, where survival was a matter of circumstance and luck. The knowledge of what capture meant — not just imprisonment but likely execution — was something every team member carried with them through every operation, every supply drop, every meeting with Maquis commanders in exposed farmhouses and forest clearings.

It did not stop them. Of the ninety-three teams inserted into France, the overwhelming majority completed their missions and survived. The operations they coordinated — the rail cuts, the bridge demolitions, the arms drops that put weapons in the hands of tens of thousands of resistance fighters — contributed to a disruption of German military movement and logistics that the Allied conventional campaign depended on in ways that are still not fully appreciated.

The Jedburgh program ended officially in the autumn of 1944 as Allied forces swept across France and the resistance emerged from the shadows into something like a conventional military force. The teams that had been operating for months in the field were withdrawn, debriefed, and redeployed — many of them to other theaters where the same skills were needed.

What they left behind was a France that had been shaped, in ways both visible and invisible, by what they had done. The Maquis fighters they had armed and advised had not won the war — that was beyond the capacity of any guerrilla force, however brave. But they had made the winning of it materially easier, at a cost in Allied lives and resources that was a fraction of what conventional military operations against the same targets would have required.

The three men in uniform, dropping blind into the French night with a radio set and a mandate and nothing else, had done what they were sent to do. Not perfectly, not without loss, not without the chaos and improvisation and near-disaster that were the inevitable companions of irregular warfare. But they had done it.

That was enough.

The Republic That Lasted Three Weeks

The Vercors Uprising

There are places that seem made for resistance. The Vercors Plateau is one of them.

Rising abruptly from the floor of the Rhône Valley southwest of Grenoble, the Vercors is a great limestone massif — a natural fortress of vertical cliffs, dense forest, and narrow gorges that has resisted easy access for as long as people have lived in its shadow. Its roads in 1944 were few and easily defended. Its forests were deep enough to hide an army. Its villages — Vassieux-en-Vercors, Saint-Martin-en-Vercors, La Chapelle-en-Vercors — were small and close-knit, their populations bound by generations of shared life in an isolated and demanding landscape. If you were going to build a stronghold in occupied France, you could not have designed a better one.

The men of the Vercors Maquis had been building exactly that since 1942. Under the leadership of figures like Eugène Chavant — a former café owner and committed socialist who became the civilian head of the Vercors resistance — and a succession of military commanders of whom the most important was Narcisse Geyer, a former French cavalry officer, the plateau had been transformed into the most ambitious and carefully planned resistance stronghold in all of occupied France. There were training camps hidden in the forests. There were weapons caches, medical facilities, communications networks, administrative structures. There was, in embryo, the skeleton of a functioning military force waiting for the weapons and the moment that would bring it to life.

The weapons were slow in coming. The moment when it arrived, came faster than anyone was ready for.

The Vercors plan — known to its architects as the Plan Montagnards, the Mountain Plan — was built around a specific and carefully considered strategic concept. The plateau would not be activated prematurely. It would not declare itself or expose its strength until the Allied invasion of France had begun and Allied forces were close enough to provide support — airborne reinforcement, supply drops, and eventually linkup with conventional ground forces pushing northward from a landing in southern France. The Vercors would become a liberated zone, an airhead, a base from which the Allies could operate against the German rear. The plan had been discussed with SOE, presented to Allied command in London and Algiers, and received what the Vercors leaders understood to be endorsement and commitment.

What exactly was promised, by whom, and in what terms is the central disputed question of the entire Vercors story.

What is documented is this: the Vercors leaders received encouragement from multiple Allied sources. Messages from London and Algiers spoke of support, of airborne operations, of the plateau's strategic importance to Allied plans for southern France. A mission from Algiers — the Eucalyptus mission, led by an American OSS officer named Major Vernon Hoppers — arrived on the plateau in June 1944 and was understood by the Vercors leadership as a concrete sign of Allied commitment. Supply drops had been promised, and some had been delivered — though never in the quantities the Maquis needed.

On June 6, 1944, the Allied landings at Normandy triggered the activation of resistance networks across France. On the Vercors, as across the rest of the country, the BBC broadcast its coded signals, and the Maquis went into action. Road ambushes were laid. German vehicles were attacked. The plateau sealed its approaches and began operating as what its leaders had always intended it to become — a liberated zone within occupied France.

The Maquis of the Vercors at this point numbered somewhere between three and four thousand fighters — a substantial force by the standards of French resistance groups, but one that was critically underequipped. Many men had weapons. Many did not. The heavy weapons — mortars, artillery, anti-aircraft guns — that would be needed to defend the plateau against a serious German attack did not exist on the Vercors in any meaningful quantity. The leaders knew this. They sent urgent requests to Algiers for the weapons and airborne reinforcement they believed had been promised.

The requests went unanswered.

On July 3, 1944, the Vercors leadership made the decision that has been debated ever since. At a ceremony in the village square of Saint-Martin-en-Vercors, before a crowd of fighters and civilians, the Free French Republic of the Vercors was formally proclaimed. The tricolor was raised. The Marseillaise was sung. In a France that had been under the boot of occupation for four years, it was an act of extraordinary defiance and hope.

It was also, as events would prove, premature by weeks or months that the plateau did not have.

The Germans had been watching the Vercors. They could not have missed it — a fortified plateau the size of a small country, openly declaring itself liberated French territory, was not an inconspicuous development. The German military command in southern France had been planning its response since June, assembling the forces and the specific tactical elements that would be needed to crack what they recognized as a serious and well-prepared defensive position.

What they assembled was overwhelming.

On July 21, 1944, the German assault on the Vercors began. It came from multiple directions simultaneously — ground forces attacking the road approaches to the plateau from north, south, east, and west, supported by artillery that outranged anything the Maquis possessed. The defenders fought hard. At the narrow gorges and road approaches where the terrain gave them the greatest advantage, Maquis units held their positions against forces many times their strength, inflicting casualties that spoke to the quality of their preparation and the ferocity of their resistance.

Then the gliders came.

On the morning of July 21 — the same day the ground assault began — German DFS 230 gliders appeared over the plateau and began landing directly on and around the village of Vassieux-en-Vercors. The troops they carried were Waffen-SS — elements of the SS-Polizei regiment, battle-hardened and operating under orders that left no room for restraint. The glider landing bypassed the defensive positions that the Maquis had spent months preparing at the plateau's approaches. There was nothing between the SS troops and the villages of the Vercors interior.

The plateau's defenders had no answer for it. They had prepared for an enemy that would have to fight its way up the roads. An enemy that landed from the sky in the middle of their position was a contingency their resources — however carefully husbanded — could not meet.

What followed in Vassieux-en-Vercors was a massacre.

The SS troops who landed by glider moved through the village with systematic brutality. Civilians who had not fled — the elderly, the sick, those who had simply nowhere to go — were killed. Houses were burned. The village that had been the geographic heart of the Vercors republic was destroyed with a thoroughness that went well beyond military necessity and into the territory of deliberate terror.

At the Vercors field hospital — a makeshift medical facility established in a grotto near the village of La

Chapelle-en-Vercors — German troops killed wounded resistance fighters in their beds and murdered several of the medical staff who had remained to care for them. Dr. Françoise Bernhard, a Jewish physician who had refused to abandon her patients when the German assault began, was among those killed.

The resistance on the plateau effectively collapsed within days of the assault's beginning. Maquis units that had not been destroyed in the fighting scattered into the forests and the surrounding mountain ranges, breaking into small groups that moved by night and hid by day, hunted by German forces conducting sweeps of the surrounding terrain. Many were caught. Many were killed. Some survived — sustained by the landscape that had always been the plateau's greatest defense and by the help of local people who continued to shelter them at enormous personal risk.

Eugène Chavant, the plateau's civilian leader, escaped. In the aftermath of the plateau's fall, he sent a message to Algiers that became one of the most raw and painful documents in the entire history of the French Resistance. He called those who had failed to send the promised support criminals and cowards. The message was received. No one in authority responded to it directly.

The accounting of what the Vercors cost is not difficult to compile. Approximately 840 people died in the uprising and its immediate aftermath — fighters killed in combat, wounded men murdered in the field hospital, and civilians killed in the reprisals that followed the plateau's fall. The village of Vassieux-en-Vercors was almost entirely destroyed. The farms and hamlets of the plateau interior were burned, their livestock killed, their inhabitants displaced.

Against this must be set what the Vercors achieved — and it achieved more than the bare narrative of its defeat suggests.

For six weeks, a resistance force of three to four thousand fighters held and administered a territory the size of a small French department, tying down German forces that were needed elsewhere. The German assault that finally destroyed the plateau required approximately 10,000 troops — Wehrmacht infantry, Waffen-SS, and specialized mountain units — along with artillery, air support, and the glider force. These were resources that the German command in southern France was diverting from other tasks at a moment when Allied pressure was building across the entire theater.

The Maquis fighters of the Vercors damaged German forces at every approach point to the plateau in the days before the assault succeeded. They inflicted casualties. They delayed. They demonstrated, in the most demanding possible circumstances, what organized resistance could accomplish against an occupying force that held every material advantage.

And they survived — enough of them survived — to continue fighting. Many of the men who scattered from the plateau in late July 1944 rejoined resistance units in the surrounding region, participated in the liberation of Grenoble in August, and went on fighting until the war ended.

The question of whether the Vercors leadership was cynically misled by Allied command — promised support that was never seriously intended — or whether it made a tragic miscalculation based on signals that were genuinely ambiguous, remains unresolved and perhaps unresolvable.

What cannot be argued is that the men and women of the Vercors deserved better than they received. They had done what they were asked to do — prepared, organized, waited, and when the signal came, fought. They had held their ground against odds that would have broken less determined people. They had built, for six extraordinary weeks, something that had not existed in occupied France since June 1940: a piece of free French territory, administered by French people, defended by French fighters, flying the French flag.

The Germans destroyed it. But they could not destroy what it had meant, or what the people who built it had shown was possible.

The survivors of the Vercors knew that. They carried it with them for the rest of their lives — the grief and the pride inseparably tangled, impossible to separate, defining everything that came after.

That is what resistance costs. That is also what it is worth.

The Man Who United the Resistance

Jean Moulin's Final Mission

He kept a sketchbook. In the margins of the war — in the brief spaces between meetings that could get him killed, in the safe houses and borrowed rooms and clandestine apartments that constituted his world — Jean Moulin drew. Portraits, mostly. Faces that caught his attention. He had trained as an artist before the war pulled him into other things, and the habit stayed with him through everything that followed, a small persistent claim on the part of himself that the war had not yet consumed.

It is worth knowing this about Jean Moulin before anything else — before the titles and the missions and the mythology that accumulated around him in death and that can make it difficult to see the man underneath. He was not born a hero. He was a prefect, a civil servant of the French Republic, a man of the moderate left who believed in democracy and legality and the institutions of the state he served. He was also, by multiple accounts, charming, funny, fond of good wine and good company, and possessed of a gift for human connection that would prove, in the extraordinary circumstances of occupied France, to be as valuable as any weapon.

He was forty-three years old when he went back into France for the last time. He had perhaps six months to live.

Jean Moulin's path to his final mission began with a knife.

In June 1940, as the German occupation began and French officials were being pressed to collaborate with or at minimum accommodate the new order, Moulin — then prefect of Eure-et-Loir, one of the most senior civilian officials in his region — refused to sign a document the Germans placed before him. The document was a lie: it attributed atrocities committed by German troops against French civilians to Senegalese soldiers in the French army. Moulin would not put his name to it.

The Germans arrested him and subjected him to treatment that left him with a certainty he carried for the rest of his life: that accommodation with the occupation was impossible, and that resistance, whatever its cost, was the only morally coherent response to what France was living through. Before his treatment ended, he attempted suicide with a piece of broken glass, cutting his own throat rather than risk that continued pressure might break him. He survived. He wore a scarf for the rest of his life to cover the scar.

He was released, eventually, and dismissed from his post by the Vichy government — which suited him perfectly. By late 1940 he was already making contact with nascent resistance groups and beginning to think through the problem that would define his remaining years: how to turn a scattered collection of independent, fractious, ideologically diverse resistance movements into something that could actually affect the outcome of the war.

The answer, he concluded, required going to London.

Moulin reached London in October 1941, after a clandestine journey through Spain and Portugal that had taken months to arrange. He came bearing a report on the state of the French resistance — the first comprehensive document of its kind to reach de Gaulle's Free French headquarters — and a set of proposals for how the resistance might be organized, unified, and supported.

De Gaulle recognized immediately what Moulin represented and what he could do. The Free French general's political position depended on his ability to claim genuine leadership of French resistance to the occupation — not merely the leadership of French forces fighting in exile, but the moral and political authority that came from representing the France that was suffering and fighting within its own borders. To make that claim credibly, de Gaulle needed the resistance movements inside France to acknowledge his leadership. To make them do that, he needed someone who could go among them and forge the necessary agreements.

He needed, in other words, exactly the kind of man Jean Moulin was.

Moulin was parachuted back into France in January 1942 with a mandate from de Gaulle and a title — National Delegate, the general's personal representative to the internal resistance — that carried authority but no coercive power whatsoever. He could not order the resistance movements to unify. He could not compel their leaders to accept de Gaulle's authority or subordinate their organizations to a common structure.

He could only persuade. Given what the resistance leaders were like, this was not a small challenge.

The French resistance of 1942 was not a single thing. It was a collection of organizations that had grown up independently, shaped by geography, ideology, personal history, and the particular circumstances of the region in which each had developed. In the southern zone — nominally governed by Vichy — the three largest movements were Combat, Libération-Sud, and Franc-Tireur. Each had its own leadership, its own structure, its own newspaper, its own vision of what France should look like after the liberation. Their leaders were strong personalities who had survived and built their organizations in conditions of extreme danger, and they did not naturally defer to anyone.

Combat was led by Henri Frenay — a former army officer of the right, intensely patriotic, deeply suspicious of the Communists and not much more trusting of de Gaulle, whom he regarded as a general seeking political power under the cover of patriotism. Libération-Sud was led by Emmanuel d'Astier de la Vigerie — an aristocrat turned leftist whose politics were the approximate mirror image of Frenay's. Franc-Tireur occupied a position somewhere between them.

Then there were the Communists — the Francs-Tireurs et Partisans, the FTP — who were the most disciplined and, in many ways, the most militarily effective resistance organization in France, but whose ultimate loyalty to Moscow rather than London or Algiers made them a permanent source of political anxiety for de Gaulle and his allies.

Moulin moved among all of them. He attended meetings, mediated disputes, absorbed the force of strong personalities and strong disagreements, and slowly, painstakingly, constructed the architecture of unification. He was helped by the authority de Gaulle's name carried and by the resources — money, weapons, communications equipment — that he could promise on London's behalf. He was hindered by the suspicion, the ego, and the genuine ideological differences that divided the movements he was trying to bring together.

He was also doing all of this while wanted by the Gestapo.

The Conseil National de la Résistance — the National Council of the Resistance, CNR — held its first full meeting on May 27, 1943, in a first-floor apartment at 48 rue du Four in Paris. Around the table sat representatives of eight resistance movements, six political parties, and two trade union federations — the full spectrum of French political and civil society that had refused to accept the occupation, gathered in one room for the first time.

It was, by any measure, a remarkable achievement. Moulin had taken approximately sixteen months of the most delicate and dangerous diplomatic work imaginable and produced something that had not existed before: a unified body capable of speaking with a single voice in the name of French resistance. The CNR passed a resolution recognizing de Gaulle as the leader of the French resistance and calling for the formation of a provisional government under his leadership. It was exactly what de Gaulle needed and exactly what Moulin had been sent to deliver.

It was also, almost certainly, the moment that sealed Moulin's fate.

A gathering of that significance — representing that many organizations, attended by that many people — was exactly the kind of event that German intelligence worked hardest to penetrate. The meeting at rue du Four had not been betrayed — it took place without German interference — but the network of contacts and communications that Moulin's work required him to maintain had created a web of connections that the Gestapo was working systematically to map.

Three weeks after the CNR's founding meeting, they found what they were looking for.

The meeting at Caluire — a suburb of Lyon — took place on June 21, 1943. It had been called to address the urgent question of who would replace General Delestraint, the military commander of the Secret Army, who had been arrested by the Gestapo in Paris on June 9. The meeting was organized by Raymond Aubrac, a resistance leader and engineer, and held at the home of a doctor named Frédéric Dugoujon, whose medical practice provided cover — the men entering the house could present themselves as patients.

Eight people attended the meeting, including Moulin. Shortly after it began, the Gestapo arrived.

The raid was swift and total. Every person in the building was arrested — including Dr. Dugoujon himself, who had no connection to the resistance and whose home had been used without his full knowledge of what the meeting was about. The men were taken to Gestapo headquarters in Lyon, which operated out of a building on the Place Bellecour under the command of Klaus Barbie — a thirty-year-old SS-Hauptsturmführer whose methods had already earned him a reputation for sadism that his subordinates found useful, and his superiors rewarded with promotions.

Several of those arrested at Caluire were eventually identified, released when their resistance connections could not be established, or transferred to other facilities. Jean Moulin was not released. The Germans knew exactly who they had.

What happened to Jean Moulin in the days following his arrest at Caluire is documented in general outline and horrible in its particulars.

Barbie's interrogation methods were not subtle. They were designed to cause maximum pain and psychological disorientation, to break the human being in front of him until whatever information he possessed became more accessible than the agony of withholding it. Moulin — who had attempted suicide four years earlier rather than risk saying under pressure what he did not wish to say — submitted to what was done to him and said nothing of operational value. The accounts of those who saw him during this period describe a man who had been beaten beyond recognition, who drifted in and out of consciousness, who was kept alive because his captors believed they had not yet extracted what he knew.

He never told them anything that mattered.

Moulin died on July 8, 1943 — either during transfer to Germany or shortly after arriving there, depending on the source. He never reached a concentration camp or a prison where his ultimate fate could be officially recorded. He simply ceased to be — the life going out of a body that had been pushed past the limit of what it could endure.

He was forty-four years old.

The question of who betrayed the Caluire meeting has been debated for more than eighty years without resolution, and it is important to treat that debate with the care it deserves — presenting what is documented, what is alleged, and what remains genuinely uncertain.

The most persistent and most seriously examined suspect has been René Hardy — a resistance leader who was present at Caluire and who, uniquely among those arrested, managed to escape from German custody almost immediately after the raid. Hardy was tried twice by French courts after the war — once in 1947 and once in 1950 — and acquitted both times. The acquittals reflected the evidentiary standard required for criminal conviction, not a historical consensus on his innocence.

The evidence against Hardy — marshaled most thoroughly by the historian Guillaume Piketty and examined in detail by multiple other researchers — includes: his presence at Caluire despite not having been originally invited, discrepancies in his account of how he came to attend, evidence that he had been in contact with the Gestapo before the meeting, and the suspicious ease of his escape from custody. No physical evidence conclusively linking him to the betrayal has been produced, and Hardy maintained his innocence until his death in 1987.

Jean Moulin was given a state funeral in December 1964, when his ashes were transferred to the Panthéon — France's memorial to its greatest citizens — in a ceremony presided over by André Malraux, de Gaulle's Minister of Cultural Affairs. Malraux's eulogy is one of the most celebrated pieces of French political oratory of the twentieth century. It ends with the image of Moulin's face as it is imagined to have appeared at the end of what was done to him at Klaus Barbie's hands — and it asks the youth of France to inherit from him what he had given everything to protect.

The monument is deserved. But monuments can flatten what they intend to honor, reducing a complex human being to a symbolic function — the martyr, the unifier, the man who held the resistance together with his bare hands until the Germans took them from him.

Jean Moulin was all of those things. He was also a man who drew faces in a sketchbook in the margins of the war, who wore a scarf to cover a scar he was not ashamed of, who moved through the most dangerous landscape in occupied Europe with a diplomat's patience and a believer's conviction.

He did not save France alone. No one person could have done that. But without what he built — the CNR, the unified command structure, the political framework that gave the resistance a coherence it had never previously possessed — the France that emerged from the occupation would have been a different and probably a darker place.

That is his monument. The institutions outlasted the man who built them. That is, in the end, the only kind of immortality that history reliably provides.

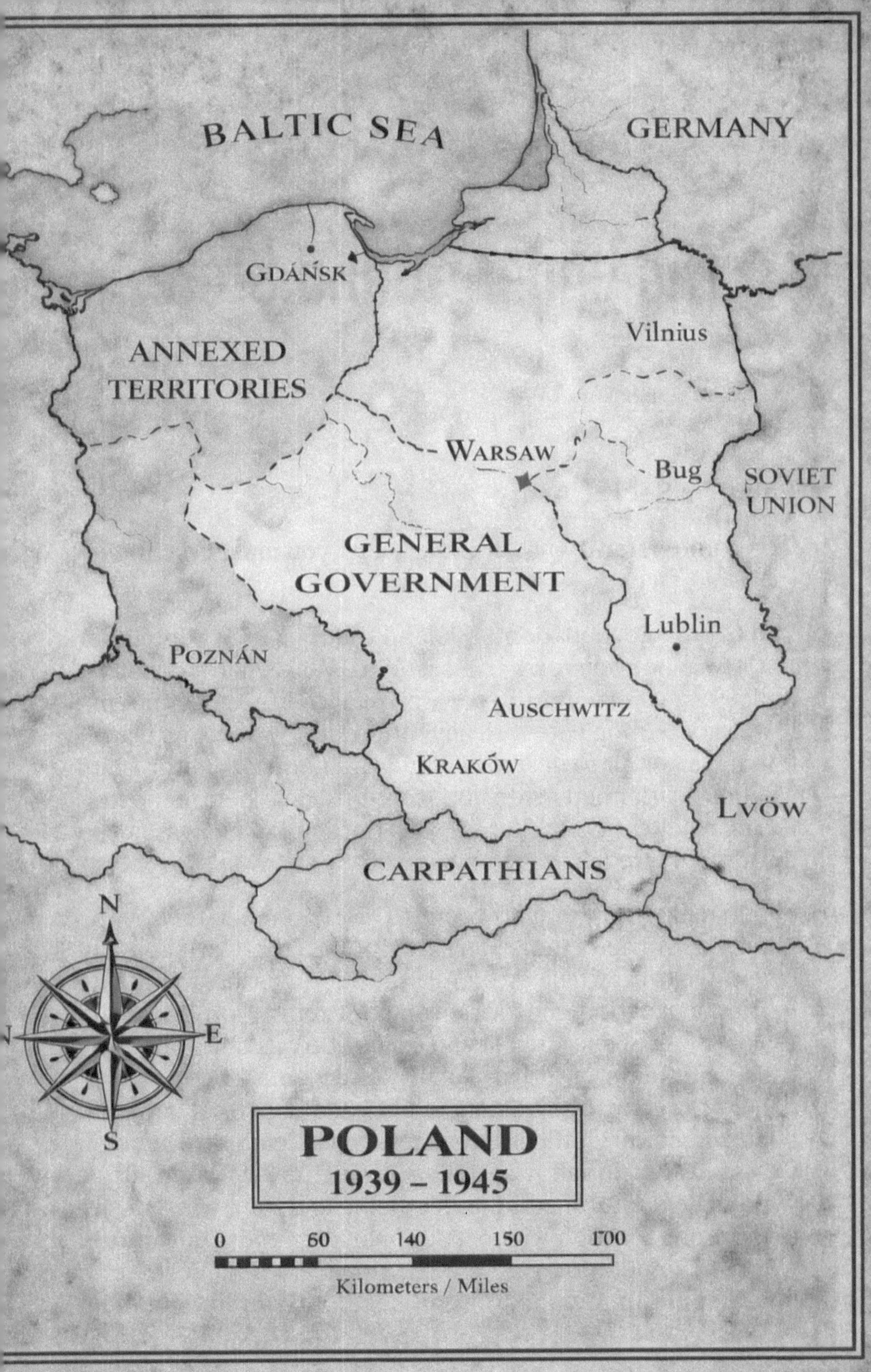

BALTIC SEA
GERMANY
GDAŃSK
Vilnius
ANNEXED
TERRITORIES
WARSAW
Bug
SOVIET
UNION
GENERAL
GOVERNMENT
Lublin
POZNÁN
AUSCHWITZ
KRAKÓW
LVÖW
CARPATHIANS
N
E
S
N
POLAND
1939 – 1945
0
60
140
150
170
Kilometers / Miles

The Underground State

Poland's Secret Army

To understand what the Poles built, you must first understand what was done to them.

The German occupation of Poland that began in September 1939 was not, even by the standards of Nazi occupation policy elsewhere in Europe, a normal military occupation. It was something categorically different — a deliberate, systematic attempt to destroy Poland as a nation, a culture, and a people. Hitler had made his intentions clear before the first German soldier crossed the Polish border. Poland was not to be administered. It was to be erased.

The machinery of erasure went to work immediately. Within weeks of the occupation's beginning, the Germans had begun what they called the AB-Aktion — Ausserordentliche Befriedungsaktion, the Extraordinary Pacification Operation — a program of mass arrest and execution targeting precisely those elements of Polish society that would be most capable of organizing resistance: professors, priests, lawyers, doctors, military officers, teachers, civic leaders. The logic was coldly rational. A people without its educated class, without its cultural and intellectual leadership, without the institutions through which a national identity is transmitted from one generation to the next, would eventually cease to be a people in any meaningful sense. It would become a reservoir of labor — expendable, replaceable, and incapable of organized resistance.

The Poles had other ideas.

What the Polish underground built in response to the occupation is, by any objective measure, one of the most extraordinary organizational achievements in the history of modern resistance. The Polish Underground State — Polskie Państwo Podziemne — was not a guerrilla army or a sabotage network, though it contained both. It was a functioning shadow government, operating in parallel with and in defiance of the German occupation authorities, providing its citizens with the institutions and services that the occupation had attempted to destroy.

It had courts. Underground tribunals administered Polish law, heard cases, issued judgments, and executed sentences — including death sentences against collaborators and informers, carried out by the resistance's own enforcement units. The Germans had abolished Polish law. The underground reinstated it, quietly and invisibly, in apartments and back rooms across occupied Poland.

It had schools. The Germans had closed Polish universities and secondary schools — higher education for Poles was explicitly prohibited, on the grounds that an educated Polish population was a dangerous one. The underground reopened them. Clandestine classes met in private apartments, in church basements, in any space that could be used without attracting German attention. Students sat their examinations and received their diplomas from institutions that existed in the eyes of the Polish government even if they had been abolished in the eyes of the German one. Thousands of students attended underground universities in Warsaw alone during the occupation years. Hundreds of professors taught them, at constant personal risk.

It had a press. Hundreds of underground newspapers and periodicals were printed and distributed across occupied Poland — a feat of organization and courage that required printing equipment to be hidden and moved constantly, distribution networks to operate invisibly, and every person involved to understand that arrest meant torture and almost certain death. The most widely distributed underground newspaper — the Biuletyn Informacyjny, the Information Bulletin — reached tens of thousands of readers at its peak, providing news uncensored by German propaganda and sustaining a sense of national community in a population that the occupation was attempting to atomize.

It had a welfare system. Underground organizations provided financial support to the families of arrested or executed resistance members, to Jews in hiding, to those who had lost their livelihoods to German economic policies. In a country where the occupiers were systematically looting the economy and reducing the population to subsistence, this was not a minor function.

And at the center of all of it, providing the military arm of the underground state, was the Armia Krajowa — the Home Army.

The Armia Krajowa — AK — grew from the merger of several earlier underground military organizations into a unified command structure that, by 1944, encompassed approximately 400,000 members across occupied Poland. It was the largest underground army in Europe — larger than the combined resistance forces of France, Yugoslavia, Greece, and every other occupied country — and it operated in conditions that made the challenges facing resistance movements elsewhere look, by comparison, almost manageable.

France had the Vichy zone, where German control was initially indirect and collaborationist authorities provided at least some buffer between the population and the occupation machinery. Yugoslavia had terrain — vast mountain ranges and dense forests where Partisan forces could operate with a degree of physical security. Poland had neither. The entire country was under direct German military and police control, with a density of occupation forces and security apparatus that left almost no physical space in which resistance could operate without the constant proximity of death.

The AK adapted to this reality with a discipline and ingenuity that its commanders had partly anticipated and partly developed through bitter experience. Compartmentalization was absolute — members knew only what they needed to know to perform their specific function. An AK courier moving documents between cells in Warsaw typically knew nothing about the cells she was connecting, the content of the messages she carried, or the structure of the organization above her immediate commander. If she was arrested — and arrest was always a possibility, on any street, at any checkpoint, at any moment — she could give the Gestapo almost nothing useful no matter what was done to her.

Weapons manufacturing was conducted in conditions that would have seemed farcical if the stakes had not been so high. The AK's technical bureau — operating from a series of constantly changing locations in Warsaw and other cities — produced functional copies of the British Sten submachine gun in small workshops hidden behind legitimate business fronts. The Polish-manufactured Sten, known as the Błyskawica — Lightning — was a remarkable achievement of clandestine engineering: a functional military weapon produced without access to specialized machinery, using materials that could be sourced without raising suspicion, by workers who had to appear to be doing something else entirely. Hundreds were manufactured and distributed to AK units across the country.

Explosives were produced similarly — small batches, widely dispersed, the production process broken into steps carried out at different locations so that no single arrest could compromise the entire operation.

The man who built the Armia Krajowa into the force it became was Stefan Rowecki — code name GROT, the Polish word for arrowhead — a professional soldier of exceptional ability whose organizational intelligence shaped the AK's structure from its earliest days. Rowecki had served in the First World War, fought in the Polish-Soviet War of 1920, and spent the interwar years studying military theory and doctrine with the systematic thoroughness of a man who understood that the next war would require capabilities that no army had yet fully developed.

When Poland fell in September 1939, Rowecki did not flee. He stayed, went underground, and began immediately to build the military organization that would become the AK. He was the architect of its command structure, its training systems, its intelligence networks, and its operational doctrine — the framework that allowed 400,000 people to function as a coherent military force while remaining individually invisible to the occupation authorities.

He was also, from the beginning, realistic about the fundamental strategic problem the AK faced. A resistance army of 400,000 people, however well organized, could not defeat the German occupation by direct military action. The AK's purpose was not to win the war — that would be done by the Allied armies advancing from east and west. Its purpose was to preserve Polish national existence through the occupation, to maintain the structures and institutions that would allow Poland to reconstitute itself as an independent state when the Germans were finally expelled, and to be ready — armed, organized, and commanded — to rise when the moment came.

That moment, when it finally arrived, would prove to be one of the great tragedies of the entire war. But that story belongs to a later chapter.

Rowecki was arrested by the Gestapo in Warsaw on June 30, 1943 — betrayed, the historical consensus holds, by an informer within the underground's circle. He was taken to Germany and held as a prisoner of considerable intelligence value, the Germans understanding that what he knew about the AK's structure and personnel was worth more if preserved than if extracted by the methods Barbie had applied to Moulin. He was executed at Sachsenhausen in August 1944, as the Warsaw Uprising — the rising he had spent years preparing for — entered its second month.

Rowecki's successor as AK commander was General Tadeusz Bór-Komorowski — BÓR, the Polish word for forest — a cavalry officer whose bearing and manner conveyed a polish that had not been much tested, before the occupation, by the specific demands of underground command. He was not

Rowecki. He lacked his predecessor's organizational genius and his instinct for the particular mathematics of resistance — for calculating what could be risked and what could not, what the organization could sustain and what would destroy it.

History has judged Bór-Komorowski primarily through the lens of the decision he made in August 1944 — the decision to launch the Warsaw Uprising, the AK's great military gamble — and the catastrophic outcome of that decision. That judgment is not the subject of this chapter. What matters here is that he inherited from Rowecki an organization of extraordinary sophistication and resilience, and that he commanded it, in the most difficult imaginable circumstances, until the rising he led was finally crushed.

The courier network that connected the Polish underground to the Polish Government-in-Exile in London was one of the most remarkable logistical achievements of the entire war.

The problem was straightforward and apparently insoluble. The underground state needed to communicate with its government in London — to report intelligence, to receive instructions, to maintain the political and operational coordination that gave the underground its legitimacy and its resources. But Poland was in the center of occupied Europe, surrounded by German-controlled territory, with no physical access to the Allied world except through a journey of extraordinary difficulty and danger.

The solution was the courier system — a network of individuals who made the journey between Warsaw and London by a route that took them through Slovakia or Hungary, into

Yugoslavia or across the Balkans, through the Middle East or across the Mediterranean, and eventually to Britain. The journey typically took months. Every leg of it was dangerous. The couriers carried documents and microfilm hidden in the soles of shoes, the bindings of books, the linings of clothing — materials that, if discovered, would mean immediate arrest and almost certain execution.

The most celebrated of these couriers was Jan Karski — a young diplomat and AK officer who made the journey to London and eventually to the United States carrying eyewitness reports of what was happening to Poland's Jewish population. Karski had been smuggled into the Warsaw Ghetto and into the Izbica Lubelska transit camp — what he later described as a camp connected to the ex-termination system — specifically so that he could provide firsthand testimony to Allied leaders. He met with Polish government ministers, British Foreign Secretary Anthony Eden, and eventually with President Franklin Roosevelt in the White House, to whom he described what he had seen with the precision and authority of a man who had been there.

The Allied leaders who received Karski's testimony did not act on it in the ways he had hoped. That failure belongs to a history larger than this book. What belongs here is the recognition of what it took to bring that testimony out of occupied Poland and into the corridors of Allied power — the courage of Karski himself, the network of people who moved him along his route, and the underground state that had created and maintained the system that made the journey possible.

The Polish Underground State existed for five years — from the first days of the occupation in September 1939 until the final suppression of the Warsaw Uprising in October 1944. During those five years it educated children, administered justice, manufactured weapons, gathered intelligence, conducted sabotage, maintained a free press, provided welfare, and sustained the national identity of a people that a totalitarian occupier was attempting to destroy.

It did all of this at a cost that is almost impossible to comprehend. The Gestapo never stopped hunting it. Every institution it built was built in the full knowledge that it could be dismantled at any moment by an arrest, a betrayal, a piece of bad luck on a Warsaw street. The people who built and maintained it — the teachers who held underground classes, the judges who administered underground law, the soldiers who manufactured weapons in hidden workshops, the couriers who carried documents across a continent under occupation — lived with that knowledge every day.

They built it anyway.

That is the fact about the Polish Underground State that resists adequate description — not the sophistication of its organization or the scale of its military arm or the reach of its courier network, impressive as all of those things were. It is the simple, stubborn, almost incomprehensible decision to build a functioning state in secret, in the middle of an occupation designed to make such a thing impossible, because the alternative — surrender, not just of territory but of national existence itself — was unacceptable.

The Germans had a word for what they intended to do to Poland. They called it *Vernichtung* — annihilation. The Polish Underground State was, at its core, a sustained and organized refusal to be annihilated.

For five years, it worked.

The Rocket in the Barn

Operation Most III

It came down on a Tuesday afternoon in late May 1944, and it came down wrong.

The V-2 ballistic missile that left its launch pad at the Heidelager test facility near Blizna in German-occupied Poland that day was supposed to follow a predictable arc — climbing to the edge of the atmosphere, following its programmed trajectory, and impacting in the designated test zone along the Bug River valley where German recovery teams waited to assess the results and collect the wreckage. The rocket program's engineers at Peenemünde and at Blizna were meticulous about these procedures. Every test firing was an opportunity to gather data, to refine the guidance systems and the propulsion characteristics that would eventually make the V-2 the most technically sophisticated weapon the war had yet produced.

This particular rocket had other ideas.

Something went wrong in the guidance system shortly after launch — precisely what has never been definitively established. The rocket deviated from its intended course, lost stability, and came down not in the designated impact zone but in the shallow waters of the Bug River near the village of Sarnaki, approximately 100 kilometers from Warsaw. It hit at a shallow angle rather than nose-first, which meant that instead of burying itself in the riverbed and destroying most of its components on impact, it came to rest in relatively shallow water with a significant portion of its structure intact.

The German recovery teams began searching immediately. They did not find it first.

The Armia Krajowa's intelligence network along the Bug River valley had been watching the German test program at Blizna for months. The AK's second bureau — its intelligence directorate — had identified the Blizna facility as a site of unusual and significant activity as early as 1943 and had tasked local units with monitoring it as closely as possible given the extreme difficulty of operating in an area with heavy German security presence. Scouts had been positioned along the likely impact zones of test rockets, with instructions to locate and report any crashed or misfired missiles before German recovery teams could secure them.

When the rocket came down near Sarnaki on that Tuesday afternoon, the local AK network was ready.

The scouts who reached the crash site first were young men — farmers' sons and village boys who knew the Bug River valley the way people know landscapes they have grown up in, which is to say completely and instinctively. They waded into the shallow water where the rocket had come to rest, assessed what they were looking at with the practical intelligence of people who understood that they did not have much time, and made a decision: they would move it before the Germans arrived.

Moving a fourteen-meter, twelve-ton rocket out of a river and into concealment without heavy equipment, in daylight, in an area under German occupation, is not a straightforward undertaking. The scouts improvised. Using farm wagons, ropes, and the labor of men who understood that the penalty for what they were doing was death, they extracted the rocket from the river and moved it to a barn on a nearby farm. Then they covered it with hay and sent word up the AK chain of command.

What they had was unclear to them in its technical specifics. What they understood with perfect clarity was that it was important.

The message that arrived at AK intelligence headquarters in Warsaw in the days following the crash set off a chain of activity that reached from occupied Poland to London in a matter of weeks. The AK's second bureau understood immediately that a largely intact V-2 rocket in Polish hands represented an intelligence opportunity of the first order — but exploiting that opportunity would require expertise, resources, and coordination that a clandestine underground army in occupied territory could only partly provide on its own.

The AK reached out to its scientific network — the constellation of Polish engineers, physicists, and technical specialists who had been operating within the underground state since the beginning of the occupation, contributing their expertise to everything from weapons manufacturing to intelligence analysis. The men who responded to the call to examine the rocket at Sarnaki represented some of the finest technical minds in Poland. They traveled to the barn in ones and twos, using cover identities and the clandestine travel arrangements that the AK had developed over years of operation, and they went to work.

The examination was conducted under conditions that tested every nerve. German search parties were active in the area from the first days after the crash — the Germans knew the rocket had come down somewhere in the Bug River valley and were determined to find it. The barn that concealed it was within the search zone. Every day the examination continued was a day in which discovery was possible, and discovery meant not just the loss of the rocket but the death of everyone connected to its concealment.

The engineers worked anyway. They documented what they found with methodical thoroughness — sketching components, noting dimensions, photographing everything that the camera they had could capture, and removing for further analysis the pieces that were small enough to transport and important enough to justify the risk. The guidance system components received particular attention. So did the propulsion elements and the fuel system — the exotic combination of liquid oxygen and ethanol that powered the rocket was itself a significant piece of intelligence, confirming and extending what British scientists had already theorized about the V-2's propulsion.

The technical report they assembled over the course of several weeks was, by any standard, a remarkable document — a detailed technical analysis of the most advanced weapons system in the world, produced under occupation conditions, by scientists working in a barn, with German search teams operating in the surrounding countryside.

The key figure in coordinating the operation on the ground was Lieutenant Jerzy Chmielewski — code name RAFAŁ — an AK officer of considerable organizational ability who served as the primary liaison between the scientific team examining the rocket and the AK command structure responsible for getting their findings to London. Chmielewski's role was logistical as much as military: keeping the examination team supplied, maintaining the security of the concealment site, managing the relationship with the local farmers whose barn and whose nerve were being tested every day, the rocket remained hidden, and coordinating the eventual transfer of materials and documentation to Warsaw.

The farmers who sheltered the rocket — and their identities have been partially but not fully established in the historical record — deserve specific acknowledgment. They were not AK soldiers. They were agricultural people who had been asked to hide a fourteen-meter German ballistic missile in their barn while German search parties combed the surrounding area, and who said yes. The specific nature of the courage this required — not the courage of action, of the soldier moving toward danger, but the courage of waiting, day after day, in the knowledge that a knock on the barn door at the wrong moment would mean death — is worth dwelling on.

They were not the only civilians whose courage made Operation Most III possible. The chain of safe houses, couriers, and ordinary Polish people who moved components, documents, and personnel across occupied territory over the weeks of the operation represented a network of complicity in which every link was a human being who had made a choice that could get them killed.

In London, the Polish Government-in-Exile's intelligence service had been working in parallel with the AK's ground operation to arrange what the intelligence made necessary: a physical extraction. The technical documentation and the selected components the engineers had removed from the rocket were valuable beyond calculation, but they were useless in a barn in the Bug River valley. They needed to reach British scientists who could analyze them properly and act on what they revealed.

The solution was Operation Most III — the third in a series of courier flights between occupied Poland and the Allied world, organized by the Polish intelligence service in coordination with the Royal Air Force. The operation required a Dakota transport aircraft to fly from an Allied-controlled airfield in Italy to a clandestine landing strip in occupied Poland, land long enough to take on cargo and passengers, and return to Italy — all in darkness, at low altitude, without fighter escort, over hundreds of miles of German-controlled airspace.

The landing strip was prepared by AK ground teams in the Tarnów area — a stretch of flat ground that had been surveyed, cleared of obstructions, and marked with signal lights that would guide the incoming aircraft. The preparation of the strip required coordination among dozens of people over several weeks, any one of whom could have compromised the operation.

The components and documentation from the V-2 examination were packaged for transport and moved from Warsaw to the Tarnów area through the AK's courier network — a journey across occupied territory that required multiple safe houses, multiple couriers, and multiple nervous nights.

The Dakota that flew Operation Most III lifted off from Brindisi in southern Italy on the night of July 25, 1944. Its crew were Polish airmen serving with the Royal Air Force — men who had escaped from Poland after the 1939 defeat, made their way to Britain through routes not unlike those traveled by resistance couriers, and spent the years since flying missions in support of the underground state they had left behind. The specific crew of the Most III flight has been identified in Polish historical records though their names appear inconsistently across different sources.

The flight north was several hours of navigating by dead reckoning over blacked-out, enemy-controlled Europe. The aircraft flew without lights, at altitudes designed to minimize radar detection, following a route planned to avoid the heaviest concentrations of German air defenses. Every mile of it was dangerous. A Dakota transport aircraft intercepted by German night fighters over occupied Poland had essentially no chance of survival.

The landing at the clandestine strip near Tarnów was the most dangerous moment of the entire operation. The aircraft came in low, guided by the signal lights of the AK reception committee on the ground, and touched down on a strip that had been prepared by hand by people who had never built an airstrip before. The landing was successful. The Dakota sat on Polish soil for less than an hour — long enough to take on the packaged V-2 components and documentation, to exchange outgoing passengers for incoming ones, and to refuel from the supply of aviation fuel the AK reception committee had somehow managed to accumulate and transport to the strip.

Then it was gone, climbing back into the darkness, heading south toward Italy and the Allied world.

When the Dakota landed in Brindisi and its cargo was examined by British scientific intelligence officers, the assessment was unambiguous. What the Polish engineers had produced — working in a barn, under occupation, with German search parties in the surrounding fields — was a technically sophisticated and operationally valuable analysis of the V-2's key systems. The guidance components, the propulsion data, the dimensional information, and the photographs gave British scientists a level of concrete, hands-on knowledge of the rocket's construction that aerial reconnaissance and signals intelligence had been unable to provide.

R.V. Jones, the scientific intelligence officer primarily responsible for analyzing German weapons programs, was among those who assessed the Polish material. His conclusion, recorded in his postwar memoir, was that the intelligence from Poland confirmed and significantly extended what British scientists had been theorizing about the V-2 on the basis of incomplete information, and that it advanced their understanding of the weapon's capabilities and limitations in ways that informed both the Allied bombing campaign against V-2 production facilities and the development of countermeasures.

The V-2 campaign against Britain — the bombardment of London and Antwerp that began in September 1944 — killed thousands of people and caused enormous damage. What it might have achieved had British scientists not had the Polish intelligence to work with, had the guidance systems and production methods of the rocket remained opaque for longer, is a counterfactual that cannot be answered with certainty. What can be said with certainty is that the Polish contribution to understanding the V-2 was real, significant, and achieved at a cost in personal courage that the British scientists working in their laboratories never had to pay.

The farmers whose barn had sheltered a German ballistic missile for several weeks watched the AK teams remove the last traces of its presence and return their land to them. Whether they knew exactly what it was they had been hiding — whether the significance of the object concealed in their hay had been explained to them or simply implied — is not recorded. What is recorded is that they had sheltered it, kept their mouths shut, and survived.

In the broader accounting of Operation Most III that is perhaps the most ordinary miracle in a story full of extraordinary ones: that so many people kept so large a secret, for so many weeks, under conditions designed to make secrets impossible.

Somewhere in the Bug River valley, the shallow water closed over the place where the rocket had rested and showed no sign of what had been there. The Germans, having searched and found nothing, eventually concluded that their missing test rocket had been destroyed in the impact or had sunk beyond recovery in the river. They filed their reports and moved on to the next test firing.

The intelligence that would help defeat the weapon they were developing was already in Britain.

Death of a Butcher

The Assassination of Franz Kutschera

By the autumn of 1943, the people of Warsaw had learned to listen for trucks.

The sound of German military vehicles moving through the city's streets in the early morning hours had acquired a specific and terrible meaning. It meant that sometime in the hours before dawn, the Gestapo or the SS had conducted one of its regular sweeps — rounding up Poles from their homes, from the streets, from wherever they happened to be when the net closed — and that the men and women collected in those sweeps were now being transported to one of the sites the Germans used for public execution. Szucha Avenue. The ruins of the Ghetto. The Pawiak prison courtyard. The locations varied. What happened at them did not.

The executions were public by design. That was the point. The Germans posted notices on the walls of Warsaw's buildings — crude printed announcements listing names, or sometimes simply numbers, of Poles who had been shot in reprisal for resistance activity. The notices were meant to terrorize. They were meant to demonstrate that the occupation had the power to take any life, at any time, for any reason or no reason at all, and that resistance to its authority would be paid for not just by those who resisted but by whoever happened to be available when the bill came due.

By the time Franz Kutschera arrived in Warsaw in September 1943 to take command of the SS and Police in the Warsaw District, the executions were already a regular feature of life in occupied Warsaw. Under Kutschera they became something else entirely — a systematic, high-frequency campaign of public murder that turned the streets of the city into an open-air theater of terror.

Franz Kutschera was thirty-nine years old when he came to Warsaw — an Austrian-born SS officer who had risen through the ranks of the SS security apparatus with the combination of ideological commitment, administrative ability, and casual brutality that the organization rewarded. He was not a battlefield soldier. He was a policeman in the SS mold — a man whose professional expertise lay in the control and suppression of civilian populations, and who brought to Warsaw a philosophy of occupation that left no ambiguity about its intentions.

His method was simple. The Armia Krajowa had been conducting sabotage operations, assassinations of collaborators and informers, and attacks on German personnel with increasing frequency and effectiveness. Kutschera's response was to make the cost of each such action so catastrophically high — in civilian lives — that the resistance would be forced to choose between fighting and allowing the innocent people of Warsaw to be massacred in their place.

The street executions began almost immediately after his arrival and escalated steadily through the autumn and winter of 1943. Groups of Poles — sometimes dozens, sometimes more than a hundred — were publicly shot in reprisal for AK operations. The names of the executed were posted on the walls. The bodies were sometimes left where they fell for hours, to ensure that as many people as possible saw them. The psychological impact on the civilian population was profound and deliberate.

By the end of 1943 Kutschera's executions had killed thousands of Warsaw's inhabitants. He had become, in the daily consciousness of the city's people, a figure of almost mythological menace — the man who decided each morning how many Poles would die that day.

The Armia Krajowa's leadership looked at what Kutschera was doing and faced one of the most agonizing decisions of the entire occupation: whether to kill him.

The decision to authorize Operation Kutschera — the AK's code name for the assassination mission — was not made quickly or easily. The debate within the AK's command structure reflected the fundamental moral paradox at the heart of resistance warfare: that action against the occupier invited reprisals against civilians, and that inaction in the face of atrocity was itself a form of complicity.

The argument against proceeding was straightforward and serious. The Germans had established a clear and consistently applied formula: for every German officer killed, a significant number of Polish civilians would be executed in retaliation. Kutschera's own pattern of reprisal killings demonstrated that this was not an idle threat. Killing him would provoke a response. People who had nothing to do with the assassination — people picked at random from Warsaw's streets and buildings — would die because of it.

The argument for proceeding was equally serious. Kutschera's campaign of public executions was itself killing hundreds of people every week — people chosen as randomly as any reprisal victims, swept up in dawn raids and shot in the streets to maintain the psychological pressure of the occupation. If his campaign was allowed to continue unchecked, the eventual death toll would dwarf whatever reprisals an assassination provoked. And there was a less quantifiable argument as well: that allowing Kutschera to continue his work without consequence was its own form of defeat, a signal to the occupation authorities and to Warsaw's civilian population that the AK could not protect or avenge the people it claimed to represent.

The AK's commander, General Bór-Komorowski, authorized the operation. The decision was, by his own later account, one of the most difficult he made during the entire war.

Planning was assigned to the AK's Kedyw — the directorate of sabotage and special operations, the unit responsible for the most demanding and dangerous missions in the AK's operational portfolio. The operation commander was Bronisław Pietraszewicz, code name LOT — the Polish word for flight — a twenty-four-year-old AK officer whose combination of operational ability and personal courage had marked him for exactly this kind of mission.

What Pietraszewicz and his team faced first was a surveillance problem of considerable complexity.

To kill Franz Kutschera, they needed to know his movements — where he went, when he went there, by what route, with what escort, in what vehicle, at what level of personal security. They needed to know this in enough detail to construct an operation that could be executed in the streets of a city under German occupation, in daylight, against a target who was protected by SS bodyguards and who moved by armored car.

The surveillance operation that preceded the assassination took several months. AK scouts — some of them very young, some of them women, all of them trained to observe without being observed — mapped Kutschera's daily routine with patient thoroughness. They identified his route from his residence on Szucha Avenue to his office at the SS and Police headquarters. They noted the timing of his movements, the number and disposition of his bodyguards, the vehicles he used, the points along his route where he was most vulnerable.

The female couriers of the AK played a critical role in this surveillance phase. Women could move through the streets of occupied Warsaw with somewhat less risk of random arrest than men — the Germans' primary suspicion fell on males of military age, who were subject to document checks and press-gang sweeps in ways that women generally were not. AK women became expert at the particular art of surveillance in plain sight — standing at a bus stop, shopping in a market, walking a familiar route — while gathering the intelligence their organization needed.

The specific woman most credited with sustained surveillance of Kutschera's movements was Elżbieta Dziembowska — code name ZO — who spent weeks observing his patterns from positions in the streets around his headquarters and residence, building the picture of his daily routine that the planning team needed. She was twenty-one years old.

By January 1944 the planning team had what it needed. A location, a timing, and a method.

The operation was set for the morning of February 1, 1944.

Kutschera's armored Mercedes followed the same route each morning — from his residence on Szucha Avenue to SS headquarters, a short journey through the streets of central Warsaw that took him past a stretch of road the planning team had identified as the optimal point for an ambush. The street was busy enough that the assault team could approach it without attracting immediate attention, but the road geometry was such that Kutschera's vehicle would be briefly constrained — unable to accelerate or maneuver — at the critical moment.

The assault team numbered approximately ten people. Pietraszewicz commanded. His fighters included Michał Issajewicz — code name MIŚ — Zbigniew Gęsicki — code name JUNO — and several other young AK soldiers whose names appear in the Polish historical record with the precision of people who deserve to be individually remembered. The female couriers — including Marianna Strybel, code name HANKA — were positioned along the escape routes, responsible for passing signals and providing cover in the aftermath of the attack.

They were armed with pistols, Sten guns, and grenades. They were, on average, in their early twenties. They had been briefed thoroughly on what was going to happen and what the risks were. Several of them had been told, as directly as the briefing process allowed, that they might not come back.

At approximately nine in the morning, Kutschera's Mercedes turned into the ambush street.

The attack lasted less than three minutes.

The assault team closed on the vehicle from multiple directions simultaneously. The bodyguard vehicles — one preceding the Mercedes, one following — were engaged immediately to prevent their occupants from intervening. Kutschera's Mercedes was forced to a stop. The SS-Brigadeführer was hit multiple times by gunfire and pulled from the vehicle.

The fighting was close and savage. In the chaos of the attack, several AK fighters were wounded by return fire from Kutschera's bodyguards. The extraction — moving the assault team away from the scene before German reinforcements arrived — was the most dangerous phase of the operation, and it was here that the heaviest costs were paid.

Pietraszewicz — LOT — was critically wounded during the extraction. He died of his wounds later that day. He was twenty-four years old. Michał Issajewicz was also critically wounded and died within hours. Two other members of the assault team were wounded seriously enough to require immediate medical attention, which in the context of occupied Warsaw meant treatment in clandestine AK medical facilities by doctors who were themselves operating in violation of German regulations.

Franz Kutschera died of his wounds before reaching a German military hospital. The operation had achieved its objective.

The German reprisal came within hours.

In the immediate aftermath of Kutschera's assassination, German security forces conducted sweeps of the streets near the attack site, arresting anyone who happened to be in the area. Over the following days, 300 Polish prisoners held at the Pawiak prison — men and women who had been arrested in previous sweeps and had no connection whatever to the assassination — were executed. Their names were posted on the walls of Warsaw in the now-familiar format of the occupation's accounting.

Three hundred lives. The AK's leadership had anticipated reprisals. They had tried to calculate the moral arithmetic in advance — weighing the ongoing death toll of Kutschera's street executions against the reprisal deaths that his killing would provoke. The calculation had led them to authorize the operation.

Whether it was the right calculation is not a question that submits to a clean answer. The 300 people executed at Pawiak in the days after Kutschera's death were murdered because of a decision they had no part in making. That is a fact, and it cannot be softened. Kutschera's successor proved somewhat less systematically murderous in his use of public street executions, and the total death toll of his tenure was lower than the trajectory of Kutschera's campaign suggested his would have been. That is also a fact, though projecting what Kutschera would have done had he lived involves a degree of speculation that honest history must acknowledge.

Bronisław Pietraszewicz — LOT — was buried in a secret location by the AK, the location of his grave kept from the Germans who would have desecrated it. He was posthumously promoted and decorated by the Polish Government-in-Exile. He had been a student before the war — a young man whose life had been interrupted by an occupation that left him, like tens of thousands of young Poles, no acceptable choice but to fight.

The other AK fighters who died in Operation Kutschera were similarly young — similarly interrupted. They had planned an operation of extraordinary tactical complexity and executed it in broad daylight against a heavily guarded target in an occupied city, and they had succeeded at the cost of their own lives. Whatever one concludes about the moral calculus that authorized their mission, the courage it required is not in question.

The women who supported the operation — the couriers and observers who had spent months in the streets of Warsaw gathering the intelligence that made it possible — returned to the work they had been doing before, because the work was not finished and there was no one else to do it. Elżbieta Dziembowska continued her AK service. So did Marianna Strybel. Their names appear in the records of the operation with the same matter-of-fact precision as the names of the fighters who carried the weapons.

The ethical weight of Operation Kutschera has not lightened with the passage of time. It sits in the historical record as a demonstration of the impossible choices that resistance warfare imposed on the people who conducted it — choices in which every available option carried a human cost, and in which the decision-maker could never be fully certain that the cost they chose was lower than the one they had avoided.

The AK's leadership made their decision with the information available to them, in the full knowledge of what a German reprisal would mean, and they made it because they had concluded that allowing Kutschera's campaign to continue unchallenged was — strategically, morally, and in terms of the plain arithmetic of death — worse than killing him.

History has not universally endorsed that conclusion. History rarely endorses the conclusions of people who make decisions in conditions of genuine moral complexity, because the distance of time makes the costs visible in ways that the pressures of the moment did not allow. What history can do — and what this account attempts to do — is hold the full weight of what happened without flinching from either the tactical achievement or the human cost.

Kutschera was dead. Three hundred prisoners were dead. The streets of Warsaw were quieter for a few weeks.

The occupation continued.

The Volunteer

Witold Pilecki Walks Into Auschwitz

There is a particular kind of courage that has no adequate name.

There is the courage of the soldier who advances under fire — fear overcome by training, by the presence of comrades, by the momentum of battle. There is the courage of the resistance fighter who carries a weapon into a city under occupation, who knows the risk and accepts it as the price of the work. These are not small things. They are extraordinary things, and the people who demonstrate them deserve every measure of recognition that history can provide.

And then there is the courage of Witold Pilecki, who in September 1940 walked deliberately into a German street roundup in occupied Warsaw, allowed himself to be arrested, and was transported to the newly established concentration camp at Auschwitz — voluntarily, with forged identity documents concealing his real name, carrying a mission from the Armia Krajowa to organize resistance from within the camp and smuggle intelligence about it to the outside world.

He knew what Auschwitz was. Or rather, he knew what it was at the moment he entered it — a brutal and murderous prison camp for Polish political prisoners, already acquiring a reputation for conditions and treatment that made survival a matter of luck as much as endurance. He could not have known what it would become, because what it became in the years that followed his entry was something that the human mind, encountering it for the first time, could not fully accommodate.

He stayed for 947 days.

Witold Pilecki was thirty-nine years old when he walked into the roundup on Żytnia Street in Warsaw on the morning of September 19, 1940. He was a cavalry officer, a landowner, a husband and father of two children, and a man whose sense of duty had been formed in a tradition of Polish patriotism that predated the current war by generations. His family had participated in earlier Polish uprisings against Russian occupation. Service to Poland — at whatever cost — was not an abstraction to him. It was an inheritance.

He had been one of the founding members of the Secret Polish Army, one of the earliest underground military organizations in occupied Poland, and he had arrived at the idea of a voluntary Auschwitz mission through the straightforward logic of an intelligence problem: the AK needed to know what was happening inside the camp, needed to have an organized network within it capable of gathering and transmitting that information, and needed to have someone reliable enough to build such a network in conditions of extreme danger. He proposed himself. After a period of consideration — the AK leadership understood what they were approving — his mission was authorized.

The forged identity documents he carried identified him as Tomasz Serafiński — a common enough name, with a cover story carefully constructed to survive the level of scrutiny German camp administrators would apply to new arrivals. He was processed with the other men caught in the roundup, loaded onto a transport, and arrived at Auschwitz with prisoner number 4859 tattooed on his forearm.

He was no longer Witold Pilecki. He would have to remember that every day, for the next two and a half years.

The Auschwitz that Pilecki entered in September 1940 was not yet the industrialized killing complex it would become. It was a camp of approximately 15,000 prisoners — primarily Polish political prisoners, intellectuals, and military officers — housed in converted Polish army barracks, subjected to conditions of deliberate brutality that the SS commandant Rudolf Höss and his staff had designed to break human beings as efficiently as possible.

The conditions Pilecki documented in the reports he would eventually smuggle out were precise and devastating. Starvation rations — a daily intake calibrated to keep prisoners alive long enough to perform forced labor while steadily destroying their physical reserves. Roll calls that lasted for hours in all weather, standing at attention while SS guards moved through the ranks. Beatings administered randomly and systematically, for infractions real and invented, as a mechanism of psychological control. The Stehbunker — the standing cell, a punishment in which prisoners were confined in spaces too small to do anything but stand, for days at a time.

The mortality rate in the early months of the camp was extraordinary. Men who had arrived healthy died within weeks —

of starvation, of disease, of the accumulated physical damage of conditions that the human body was not designed to sustain. The camp authorities did not regard this as a problem. It was, in the logic of the occupation's ultimate intentions for Poland, something closer to a feature.

Pilecki watched all of it with the dual consciousness of a man who was simultaneously a prisoner — suffering everything the other prisoners suffered, with no special protection and no way of revealing his real identity without destroying everything — and an intelligence officer, observing, analyzing, and recording. He was perpetually hungry, perpetually exhausted, perpetually at risk of selection for punishment or worse. He was also, throughout all of it, thinking about how to build a resistance network in conditions that made every human connection a potential source of catastrophic exposure.

The organization Pilecki built inside Auschwitz was called the Związek Organizacji Wojskowej — the Military Organization Union, ZOW — and it grew from the most careful and painstaking foundation imaginable.

He began with a single contact — a prisoner he assessed as trustworthy, reliable, and possessed of the particular psychological resilience that the work would require. From that contact he built outward, one carefully chosen addition at a time, constructing a cellular network in which each member knew only the people immediately above and below them in the structure. The principles were identical to those the AK applied in the world outside the camp — compartmentalization, need-to-know, the organizational discipline that ensured a single arrest could not unravel the whole.

Inside Auschwitz, the stakes of a security failure were even higher than in the streets of Warsaw. A prisoner identified as organizing resistance faced not just arrest but the specific brutality that the SS reserved for those who challenged the camp's authority — torture in the camp jail, followed by execution in the courtyard of Block 11, the punishment block, where a wall had been built for exactly this purpose.

Pilecki built anyway. By 1941 the ZOW had hundreds of members distributed across the camp's blocks and work details — men who shared food with the most desperate prisoners, provided moral support to those on the edge of collapse, maintained a human network of solidarity in conditions designed to reduce people to isolated atoms of survival, and gathered intelligence about everything that happened within the camp's perimeter.

Getting that intelligence out required equal ingenuity. Pilecki developed a system for passing information through prisoners who were transferred to other camps or released — a rare occurrence, but one that provided a conduit. He also used camp workers who had contact with the outside world through their labor assignments. The reports that made it through this system to the AK command in Warsaw — and eventually to the Polish Government-in-Exile in London and to Allied intelligence services — were the first detailed, first-hand accounts of Auschwitz to reach the outside world.

The intelligence Pilecki smuggled out of Auschwitz described, with the precision of a trained military observer, what was happening inside the camp. The systematic starvation. The organized beatings. The medical experiments conducted on prisoners without consent. And, as 1942 progressed and Auschwitz began its transformation into something categorically different from what it had been, the mass murder of Jewish deportees arriving by train from across occupied Europe.

The reports were received in London and in Washington. They were read by people in positions of authority — people who had the power, in theory, to act on what they contained. The responses they generated were, by the standard of what the intelligence demanded, catastrophically inadequate.

The reasons for this failure of response have been debated by historians for decades and belong to a history larger than this book. What belongs here is the simpler and more terrible fact: that Pilecki's reports were not fully believed. The scale of what he was describing — the organized industrial murder of hundreds of thousands of people — was sufficiently outside the frame of what the human mind could accommodate that even people of goodwill and intelligence found ways to discount it, to attribute it to exaggeration or propaganda, to file it in the mental category of the unverifiable and move on.

Pilecki knew, somewhere in the part of him that had continued to think and observe and record through 947 days of Auschwitz, that his reports were not producing the response they should have produced. It was one of the specific torments of his situation — to know what was happening, to have succeeded in communicating it, and to find that the knowledge was not being acted upon.

Pilecki escaped from Auschwitz on the night of April 26 to 27, 1943 — nearly two and a half years after he had voluntarily entered it.

The escape was carefully planned and required the assistance of several ZOW members and sympathetic camp workers. Pilecki and two other prisoners — Jan Redzej and Edward Ciesielski — were assigned to a night shift at the camp bakery, which had a connection to the outside perimeter that offered a possibility the others did not. They overpowered a guard, cut a telephone line, and moved through the darkness toward the camp perimeter.

The pursuit began almost immediately. German search teams with dogs covered the area around the camp in the hours after the escape was discovered. Pilecki and his companions moved by night and hid by day, travelling through the countryside south of Auschwitz toward AK contacts who had been briefed on the possibility of exactly this kind of approach. They survived the immediate pursuit, made contact with the AK network in the Kraków area, and eventually reached Warsaw.

The report Pilecki gave to AK leadership in Warsaw was the most comprehensive and detailed account of Auschwitz that any eyewitness had yet provided. It ran to dozens of pages, was precise about numbers and methods and the organizational structure of the camp's killing operations, and left no room for the kind of comfortable uncertainty that had allowed earlier reports to be set aside. He presented it to his commanders with the expectation that it would finally produce the response that his smuggled reports had failed to generate.

The response, again, fell short of what the intelligence demanded. The AK leadership forwarded the report to London. London read it. The bombing of the Auschwitz rail lines and infrastructure — one of the specific recommendations that Pilecki and others had been urging — did not happen.

Pilecki went back to fighting the war he could fight, in the city he could fight it in.

He participated in the Warsaw Uprising of August 1944 — the great and catastrophic rising of the AK that had been building since the beginning of the occupation and that ended, after sixty-three days of brutal street fighting, in the destruction of the city and the surrender of the surviving AK forces. Pilecki fought in the uprising as he had done everything — with absolute commitment and without complaint about the odds.

When the uprising collapsed and its surviving fighters were taken prisoner, Pilecki went into German captivity as a prisoner of war — a status that, under the laws of war, should have protected him. He survived the remaining months of the war in German POW camps and was liberated by Allied forces in May 1945.

He returned to Poland.

It was the decision that killed him.

The Poland that Pilecki returned to in 1945 was not the Poland for which he had volunteered to enter Auschwitz. It was a country in the process of being absorbed into the Soviet sphere of influence, its government being replaced by a Communist administration installed with Soviet backing and maintained by Soviet power. The underground state that Pilecki had served — the Polish Government-in-Exile's shadow government, the AK, the entire structure of democratic

Polish resistance — was being systematically dismantled and its members hunted by the new regime's security apparatus, the Urząd Bezpieczeństwa, the UB.

Pilecki understood what was happening. He had stayed in contact with the Polish Government-in-Exile's intelligence service after liberation, gathering intelligence on Soviet activities in Poland and transmitting it westward — an extension, in altered circumstances, of the intelligence work he had been doing since 1940. It was exactly the kind of activity that the UB was watching for.

He was arrested in May 1947.

The interrogation that followed lasted months. The UB's methods were not substantially different from those the Gestapo had applied to other people Pilecki had known — sustained physical and psychological pressure designed to extract confession and collaboration. Pilecki gave them neither in any meaningful form, though the physical toll of what was done to him was severe. He reportedly told one of his AK contacts, in a message smuggled out of custody, that Auschwitz had been nothing compared to what the UB was doing to him.

Whether this was literally true or an expression of the particular horror of being tortured by the government of the country he had sacrificed everything to defend, it speaks to the specific cruelty of his situation in a way that requires no elaboration.

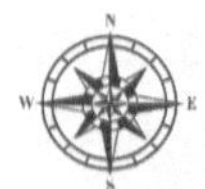

The trial of Witold Pilecki opened in Warsaw in March 1948. The charges against him — espionage, illegal border crossing, possession of weapons, and several other counts — were fabricated in their framing and distorted in their specifics, designed to fit the legal forms of the new regime's justice while destroying the man they were aimed at. The prosecution presented him as a spy and a traitor. The defense was permitted to present almost nothing.

He was convicted on all counts and sentenced to death.

The sentence was carried out on May 25, 1948. Witold Pilecki was executed by a single gunshot to the back of the head in the basement of the Mokotów Prison in Warsaw. He was forty-seven years old. His family was not told where his body was buried. They were not told for decades. The location of his remains — likely in one of the mass graves at a Warsaw cemetery where the Communist regime buried its executed prisoners — was not definitively identified until 2012, when forensic investigation produced results that Polish authorities considered sufficient for a formal identification.

Poland officially rehabilitated Witold Pilecki in 1990, following the fall of the Communist government. He was posthumously promoted to the rank of Colonel and awarded the Order of the White Eagle — Poland's highest state honor — in 2006. In 2013, the Polish parliament passed a resolution recognizing him as one of the greatest heroes in Polish history.

The rehabilitation was just. It was also, by definition, too late to mean anything to the man it honored.

What does it mean to voluntarily enter Auschwitz? What does it mean to spend 947 days in a place designed to exterminate human beings, building a resistance network, gathering intelligence, maintaining the moral coherence of a man who understood what he was doing and why, and then to escape and spend the rest of the war fighting, and then to return to a country whose new government would torture and murder you for the crime of having served your actual country too well?

It means something that the word courage does not adequately contain. The language of heroism, applied to Pilecki, feels at once entirely appropriate and somehow insufficient — as if the scale of what he did and what was done to him in return has pushed past the boundaries of what the available vocabulary can hold.

He was a man who looked at the worst thing in the world and walked into it with open eyes because someone had to, and he was the someone who was available. He was a man who built light in darkness — literally, in the ZOW network that provided solidarity and human connection to prisoners who would otherwise have faced the camp's atomizing terror entirely alone. He was a man who told the truth about what he had seen at a time when the truth was almost too large to be believed, and who was punished for it by two successive governments — the German one that had created what he described, and the Communist one that preferred its own version of history.

He deserved better from the world than the world gave him. That is, perhaps, the simplest and most complete thing that can be said about Witold Pilecki.

History, at least, has corrected its accounting.

The Fan

Striking the Eastern Front's Lifeline

In the autumn of 1941, Germany was winning the war in the east.

Operation Barbarossa — the German invasion of the Soviet Union launched on June 22, 1941 — had torn through Soviet defenses with a violence and speed that surpassed even the most optimistic projections of its planners. By October, German forces had advanced more than a thousand kilometers into Soviet territory, captured millions of prisoners, destroyed thousands of tanks and aircraft, and stood within striking distance of Moscow itself. The Wehrmacht's logistical machine — the railways, roads, bridges, and supply depots that fed fuel, ammunition, food, and replacement equipment to the armies advancing eastward — was running at a pace and scale that had no precedent in the history of warfare.

It was also running, for most of its length through occupied Poland, directly through territory controlled by the Armia Krajowa.

The British SOE had understood the strategic implications of this geography almost from the moment Barbarossa began. The supply lines feeding the German armies in the east crossed hundreds of kilometers of occupied Polish territory — territory where the AK had cells, networks, and the organizational infrastructure to conduct sustained sabotage operations. If those supply lines could be disrupted — even partially, even temporarily — the impact on German operational capacity at the front could be significant. Every train delayed, every bridge requiring repair, every fuel depot destroyed represented a subtraction from the margin of supply that kept the German advance moving.

In late 1941 SOE proposed to the AK leadership the creation of a specialized sabotage organization dedicated exclusively to attacking German supply and communication lines along the eastern front's logistical corridor. The AK agreed. The organization they built together was called the Wachlarz — the Polish word for fan — named for the shape of its operational area, which spread in a broad arc from the Baltic coast in the north to the Carpathian Mountains in the south, covering approximately 1,000 kilometers of German-controlled territory.

It would become one of the most ambitious and least celebrated sabotage operations of the entire war.

The organizational challenge the Wachlarz faced was unlike anything the AK had previously attempted. The existing AK network was built for operations in the German-occupied territories of central Poland — the General Government zone where the underground state had been developing since 1939, where the population was overwhelmingly Polish, and where years of clandestine operation had produced a mature infrastructure of safe houses, couriers, and local support.

The Wachlarz was designed to operate in a fundamentally different environment. Its operational arc extended through territories that had been part of eastern Poland before the Soviet occupation of 1939 and the German occupation of 1941 — areas with mixed Polish, Ukrainian, Belarusian, and Jewish populations, where the political situation was more complex, where the AK's existing network was thinner, and where the density of German security forces was in some areas even higher than in the General Government zone.

The solution was a structure built specifically for the task. The Wachlarz was organized into five sectors, each covering a section of the operational arc, each commanded by an officer with the authority and the resources to conduct independent operations within his sector without waiting for direction from central command. The sectors were deliberately designed to function autonomously — because the communications challenges of coordinating operations across 1,000 kilometers of occupied territory made centralized control not merely difficult but operationally dangerous. A network that depended on constant communication between its components was a network that the Germans could disrupt by targeting those communications.

Each sector maintained its own intelligence network, its own supply of weapons and explosives, its own courier system, and its own relationship with the local population — or whatever relationship with the local population the specific ethnic and political geography of its area made possible. The fighters who conducted operations were recruited locally where possible, supplemented by personnel dispatched from the AK's central resources.

The Wachlarz's commander was Major Jan Piwnik — code name PONURY, the Polish word for grim or somber — a former Polish army officer whose combination of personal courage, organizational ability, and willingness to lead from the front gave the organization the kind of leadership its demanding mission required. Piwnik was not an administrator in the SOE mold — he was a fighter, and the Wachlarz under his command reflected that character.

The railway network was the Wachlarz's primary target, and it attacked it with a consistency and variety of method that demonstrated the quality of the sabotage training its fighters had received.

Rail sabotage in the Wachlarz's operational area required solutions adapted to the specific conditions of each sector. In some areas, direct attack on the track — removing sections of rail, cutting fishplates, tampering with switches — was the primary method, carried out by small teams operating at night in terrain that offered reasonable cover for approach and withdrawal. In others, the physical exposure of the railway lines made this approach too dangerous, and the teams developed indirect methods: tampering with the track in ways that would cause derailment without requiring extended time at the target, or attacking the locomotives and rolling stock in their maintenance facilities where security was sometimes lighter than on the line itself.

The derailment operations were the most dramatic in their immediate effects and the most demanding in their execution. A derailed train — particularly a locomotive pulling a heavy military freight consist — created a disruption that extended well beyond the physical damage to the train itself. The wreckage had to be cleared before the line could be used again. Repair crews had to be brought in. The trains backed up behind the blockage had to be rerouted or held. A single well-executed derailment on a main supply line could close it for hours or days.

In the Wachlarz's first year of operations, its teams carried out dozens of such attacks across the five sectors. The Brest-Litovsk to Minsk line — one of the primary supply arteries for Army Group Center — was targeted repeatedly. So were the lines feeding Army Group South through Ukraine. Bridges — harder targets than open track but far more valuable when successfully destroyed — were attacked where the Wachlarz had the explosives and the trained personnel to do the job properly.

One of the most significant bridge operations in the Wachlarz's documented record took place in the Pinsk area in the spring of 1942, when a team from the northern sector destroyed a railway bridge over one of the river crossings on the Minsk supply line, closing the line for a period that German records — captured after the war — indicate lasted several days and required the diversion of supply traffic to secondary routes. The operation required weeks of surveillance, the acquisition and transportation of a substantial quantity of explosives through German-controlled territory, and an assault on a target that was guarded by German security forces.

All of it was done by young men in occupied territory, operating without the military infrastructure that conventional soldiers relied upon, sustained by the organizational network of the Wachlarz and by their own refusal to stop.

The fuel depot attacks were less frequent than the railway operations but potentially more strategically significant. A German armored formation without fuel was not a fighting formation — it was a collection of expensive metal sitting in a field. The Wehrmacht's consumption of fuel on the Eastern

Front was enormous and the supply chain that provided it was vulnerable at every point where it passed through occupied Polish territory.

The Wachlarz conducted attacks on fuel storage facilities in several of its sectors, using incendiary devices and direct sabotage to destroy stocks that the German military could not easily replace. The verification of the strategic impact of individual attacks is difficult — German logistics records are inconsistent, and distinguishing the contribution of any specific sabotage action from the general strain on German supply that resulted from the scale of Eastern Front operations is not straightforward. What the records do show is that German military authorities in the occupied eastern territories regarded the Wachlarz's operations as a serious problem and devoted substantial security resources to countering them — resources that had to come from somewhere and that were therefore not available for other purposes.

The attacks on communication lines — telephone cables, telegraph installations, the signals infrastructure that the German command network depended on — were the third axis of the Wachlarz's campaign. These operations were lower-profile than the railway attacks but carried out at higher frequency, because communication lines were less heavily guarded than rail infrastructure and could be disrupted by smaller teams with simpler equipment. A cut telegraph line was repaired in hours. A pattern of repeated cuts along the same route — each one requiring repair crews and security escorts to be dispatched, each one consuming time and resources — created a cumulative burden on German logistics administration that was disproportionate to the effort required to inflict it.

The territory in which the Wachlarz operated was among the most dangerous in occupied Europe for resistance activity, and not only because of the German security presence.

The ethnic complexity of the eastern Polish territories created political and operational challenges that the organization had to navigate simultaneously with its military mission. Ukrainian nationalist organizations — particularly the Ukrainian Insurgent Army, the UPA — were in active conflict with both the German occupiers and the Polish resistance in parts of the Wachlarz's operational area, creating a three-way conflict of extraordinary brutality in which Polish civilians were among the primary victims. The Wachlarz's fighters operated in areas where they could not always be certain who the enemy was, or from which direction the next threat would come.

The German counter-resistance campaign in the eastern territories was also qualitatively different from what the AK faced in the General Government zone. The security forces operating in the occupied east included not just the Gestapo and the SS but military units whose experience on the Eastern Front had stripped away whatever residual inhibitions about civilian killing they might once have possessed. The reprisal operations conducted against populations suspected of supporting the Wachlarz were savage even by the standards of German occupation policy elsewhere.

Captured Wachlarz fighters were not taken to Gestapo headquarters for interrogation and eventual transfer to a concentration camp. They were typically shot where they were found, after whatever interrogation the local security commander considered necessary. The expectation of death upon capture was not a theoretical calculation for Wachlarz fighters — it was an operational reality that shaped every decision about when to fight and when to run.

The human cost of the Wachlarz's operations mounted steadily through 1942 and into 1943, and the pattern of losses followed a trajectory that was painfully familiar from the experience of SOE's French circuits: initial operations conducted with relative impunity, followed by the gradual penetration of the organization by German intelligence, followed by arrests that compromised additional members, followed by further arrests, in a cascade that threatened to consume the organization entirely.

The first serious penetrations of the Wachlarz network began in mid-1942, when German counter-intelligence operations in the northern sector identified and arrested several members of the local courier and support network. The arrests produced intelligence — under what conditions and by what means it was extracted the record does not always specify — that allowed the Germans to identify additional members and roll up portions of the sector's operational structure.

Jan Piwnik — PONURY — survived the first wave of penetrations and continued to command the organization through the crisis, his leadership holding together what the arrests were trying to destroy. But the losses were serious. Trained saboteurs were not easily replaced. The networks of safe houses and local support that took months to build were compromised and had to be rebuilt from scratch. The explosives and weapons stocks that individual cells had accumulated were seized or had to be abandoned.

By early 1943 the cumulative effect of German counter-intelligence operations had significantly degraded the Wachlarz's operational capacity. The organization continued to function — continued to conduct rail attacks and bridge demolitions and communication line sabotage — but at a reduced tempo and with a smaller and less experienced pool of fighters than it had possessed at its peak.

Piwnik was eventually transferred from Wachlarz command to lead partisan operations in the Kielce region — an acknowledgment by the AK leadership that the Wachlarz's original operational concept required restructuring if it was to continue functioning. His replacement faced the same Gestapo pressure that had been steadily eroding the organization since mid-1942.

The assessment of what the Wachlarz achieved — against what it cost — is genuinely difficult, and honesty requires acknowledging the difficulty rather than resolving it artificially in either direction.

The strategic impact of the Wachlarz's operations on German logistics on the Eastern Front was real but not decisive. The German supply system was large, redundant, and capable of absorbing a significant level of disruption without catastrophic failure. The Wachlarz could delay trains, destroy bridges, burn fuel stocks, and cut communication lines — but it could not permanently close the supply corridors that fed the German advance, because the Germans had the engineering resources and the security forces to repair and protect their infrastructure faster than a clandestine sabotage organization could destroy it.

What the Wachlarz could do — and did — was impose a cumulative tax on German logistics that consumed time, resources, and personnel that the German military could not afford to spare. Every derailment that required a repair crew, every destroyed bridge that required an engineering battalion, every fuel depot that required a security detachment — these were subtractions from a margin of operational capacity that, on the Eastern Front, was always tighter than German planning had anticipated.

The men who paid for these subtractions with their lives were not fighting with any illusion that their individual operations would turn the tide of the war. They were fighting because the supply lines of the army that was killing their people ran through their country, and because the Armia Krajowa had asked them to do something about it, and because they had said yes.

That, in the end, is what the Wachlarz was — not a war-winning instrument, but a demonstration of what people do when the worst thing in the world is happening and they have the means and the will to resist it.

They resist it. Whatever it costs.

The Silent and Unseen

Poland's Elite Cichociemni

They had a saying in the training camps of Scotland, passed among the Polish soldiers who were preparing to go back into the country they had escaped from: that the journey to occupied Poland was easy. It was staying alive once you got there that required talent.

The saying was dark in the way that soldiers' humor is always dark — a compression of real fear into something that could be spoken aloud without breaking the speaker. The men who said it knew precisely what waited for them on the other side of the drop. They had been reading the intelligence reports from the AK. They had been briefed by people who had made the journey and come back — and by the silences around the names of people who had made it and had not. They understood, with the clarity that good training and honest briefing can produce, that what they were volunteering for was among the most dangerous things a human being could do in the second year of the Second World War.

They volunteered anyway. All of them. That was the first and most fundamental requirement of the program — that participation be entirely voluntary, at every stage, with the option to withdraw available at any point without penalty or stigma. No one was ordered to become Cichociemni. The ones who became them chose to.

Three hundred and sixteen men made that choice. Of them, one hundred and twelve did not survive the war.

The name by which they are known — Cichociemni — is Polish for silent and unseen, and it captures with precision the operational philosophy that shaped everything about how they were trained and how they worked. The silent and unseen soldier is not the soldier who advances across open ground under fire. He is the soldier who is never where the enemy expects him to be, who moves through hostile territory without leaving traces that can be followed, who strikes and withdraws before the response can be organized. He is, in the most fundamental sense, a ghost — present, effective, and invisible.

The program that produced the Cichociemni grew from the specific needs of the Armia Krajowa in 1940 and 1941. The AK was building an underground army of remarkable size and ambition, but it was doing so in isolation — cut off from the Allied world by the geography of occupation, dependent on the thin courier links that connected occupied Poland to the Polish Government-in-Exile in London for its communications and its supply. What it needed, and what it communicated urgently to London, was not just weapons and money — though it needed those too — but people. Specifically, people with skills that the occupation had made impossible to develop inside Poland: trained parachutists, wireless operators, demolitions specialists, intelligence officers, commanders who had been exposed to Allied thinking and Allied methods and who could bring that exposure back into the underground army.

The British SOE and the Polish intelligence service in London began working on the problem in 1940. The solution they developed was the Cichociemni program — a training and insertion system that would take Polish soldiers already serving with Allied forces in Britain, give them the specialized skills the AK needed, and parachute them into occupied Poland to serve in whatever capacity their training and the AK's requirements dictated.

The selection process was designed to identify not just physical capability but the specific psychological profile that clandestine operations in occupied territory required.

Physical fitness was the baseline — candidates had to meet standards that eliminated the merely fit and identified the genuinely exceptional. But physical fitness was, in a sense, the easiest part. The qualities that the selectors were really looking for were harder to assess and harder to fake: emotional stability under prolonged stress, the ability to function independently without the organizational structure and chain of command that conventional soldiers depended upon, the capacity to make good decisions with incomplete information in situations where the wrong decision meant death, and the particular kind of social intelligence — the ability to read people, to construct and maintain convincing false identities, to know instinctively who could be trusted and who could not — that clandestine work demanded above all else.

Candidates were observed over extended periods, assessed not just in formal testing but in the ordinary interactions of daily life — how they behaved under pressure, how they responded to failure, whether their judgment under stress matched their judgment at rest. Many candidates who passed the physical requirements were eliminated at this stage. The program was looking for something rare, and it was willing to accept a smaller number of graduates rather than lower the standard to increase the count.

Those who made it through the selection process entered a training regimen conducted primarily in Scotland — at facilities scattered across the Highlands that had been developed by SOE for exactly this kind of work. The curriculum covered everything the AK needed. Parachuting — conducted at RAF stations in England, requiring trainees to complete a minimum number of jumps before qualification, including night jumps in conditions as close as possible to those they would face in the field. Wireless operation — the technical skill that was in shortest supply within the AK and most urgently needed. Demolitions — the precise, practical knowledge of explosives that distinguished a saboteur who could reliably destroy a bridge from one who could merely damage it. Small arms, fieldcraft, map reading, escape and evasion. And, running through all of it, the specific training for clandestine operation in occupied territory: cover story construction, surveillance detection, resistance to interrogation, the thousand practical details of living invisibly in a society controlled by an enemy who was looking for you.

The interrogation training was, by multiple accounts, the most psychologically demanding component of the curriculum. Trainees were subjected to simulated Gestapo interrogations — conducted with sufficient realism to produce genuine stress responses — designed to identify weaknesses in their cover stories and in their psychological resilience. A trainee who broke under simulated interrogation was a trainee who might break under the real thing, and the program would rather discover that in Scotland than in Warsaw.

The mechanics of inserting a Cichociemni into occupied Poland were a feat of coordination that required the alignment of multiple elements across hundreds of miles of German-controlled airspace, and that depended at every point on things that could not be controlled: weather, German air defenses, the reliability of reception teams on the ground, and the basic willingness of the night to provide sufficient darkness.

The aircraft used for most Cichociemni insertions were Halifax or Liberator bombers modified for the parachute insertion role — their bomb bays adapted to carry supply containers alongside the agents, their ranges extended by additional fuel tanks to cover the distance from their bases in Britain or later in southern Italy to the drop zones in occupied Poland. The flight alone — several hours each way, at low altitude over German-controlled Europe, without fighter escort — was dangerous enough that some insertion missions turned back before reaching the drop zone when German air defenses made the risk unacceptable.

When conditions allowed the aircraft to reach the drop zone, the final minutes before the jump were the most demanding of the entire journey. The agent — dressed in a flight suit over his civilian cover clothing, his equipment loaded into containers that would drop alongside him — lay in the modified bomb bay or crouched at the jump hatch, waiting for the signal from the dispatcher. Below him, invisible in the darkness, the reception committee was signaling with torches — a pattern pre-arranged through AK communications with London, confirming that the drop zone was secure and the reception team was in position.

The signal came. The agent dropped.

A parachute insertion into occupied Poland at night, from a few hundred feet, in darkness, into a landscape the agent might never have seen in daylight — this is a situation that rewards either extraordinary competence or extraordinary luck, and preferably both. The landing could go anywhere: into a field, into a forest, into a river, onto a road. The reception committee could be there or, if something had gone wrong in the preceding hours, it could not. The Germans could be waiting, having intercepted the wireless communications that arranged the drop, or they could be somewhere else entirely.

The Cichociemni who landed successfully — which was most of them, most of the time — were met by AK reception teams who helped them gather their equipment, conceal the parachute, and move away from the drop zone before daylight. They were given their initial documents and cover identities, briefed on the current security situation in their area, and transferred into the AK network that would place them in their assigned roles.

For most of them, the jump was the beginning of an operational period that would last months or years — a sustained immersion in the world of clandestine resistance from which the only exits were the end of the war, capture, or death.

Jan Piwnik — PONURY — has appeared already in this book, in the chapter on the Wachlarz, which he commanded. His story belongs here as well, because he was Cichociemni before he was a Wachlarz commander — one of the first cohort of trained soldiers to be dropped into occupied Poland, arriving in December 1941 after a journey from Britain that tested the program's logistics almost to breaking point.

Piwnik's operational record in Poland illustrated the way the Cichociemni functioned at their best — not as isolated individual operators but as catalysts who accelerated and improved the operations of the larger AK networks they joined. He brought with him demolitions expertise that the Wachlarz needed, command skills that its structure required, and the particular credibility that came from having been trained alongside Allied officers and exposed to Allied operational thinking. When he led a demolitions team against a railway target, the men with him were better at their work for his presence. When he commanded a sector of the Wachlarz's arc, the sector's operations were more professional, more carefully planned, and more effectively executed than they would have been without him.

He was also, by the accounts of people who served with him, a commander in the most human sense — someone who understood that the men under his command were not instruments but people, and who led accordingly. In the particular isolation and pressure of clandestine warfare, that quality mattered more than any technical skill.

He died in June 1944, at thirty-two, in a firefight with German forces — one of the 112.

Elżbieta Zawacka — code name ZO — occupies a unique place in the history of the Cichociemni because she was the only woman among the 316. Her path to the program was as unconventional as her inclusion in it.

Zawacka had been an AK courier before her insertion training — one of the extraordinary women who maintained the underground state's communication links across occupied

Europe, making journeys of extraordinary danger with the practiced efficiency of someone who had learned, through experience, exactly how to move through hostile territory without being noticed. She had traveled from occupied Poland to the west multiple times, carrying intelligence and communications for the AK and the Polish Government-in-Exile, before being selected for the Cichociemni training program.

Her training followed the same curriculum as the male candidates, with the same standards and the same expectations. She qualified as a parachutist, as a wireless operator, and in the full range of clandestine skills the program covered. She was dropped back into Poland in September 1943 — jumping from a Halifax into the darkness over occupied territory, landing successfully, and disappearing into the AK network with the same invisibility that the program's name described.

Her operational role inside Poland drew on the full range of her skills — courier work, intelligence transmission, the organizational functions that the AK's communications network depended on. She survived the war, survived the Communist period — though not without difficulty; she was arrested by the UB in 1951 and held for three years before being released — and lived to see Poland's independence restored. She died in 2009 at the age of ninety-nine, the last surviving Cichociemni.

Aleksander Tarnawski — code name UPŁAZ — represents a third and different kind of Cichociemni story: the specialist whose particular technical skill was the primary reason for his insertion, and whose operational record illustrated the way the program functioned as a delivery mechanism for capabilities the AK could not develop internally.

Tarnawski was a demolitions specialist — trained to a standard that the AK's own internal resources could not match, capable of working with the full range of British explosive materials and techniques that SOE's supply network was providing to the resistance. His insertion in 1943 placed him in the AK's Kedyw — the sabotage directorate that conducted the most demanding special operations in the underground army's portfolio, including the Kutschera assassination described in a previous chapter.

His operational record included railway demolitions, attacks on German military installations, and the training of AK demolitions teams — the multiplication function that made the Cichociemni program more than the sum of its individual participants. Each Cichociemni who trained AK fighters in the skills he had brought from Britain was extending the reach of those skills beyond his own individual capacity. A demolitions specialist who trained fifty AK saboteurs in the proper use of plastic explosive had done something more valuable than fifty individual demolitions operations, because he had created a capability that would outlast his own presence in the field.

That multiplication function was, arguably, the most important thing the Cichociemni program accomplished — not the individual operations its graduates conducted, significant as those were, but the systematic upgrading of the AK's technical capabilities across every area that the program's training covered.

The statistical reality of the Cichociemni is worth sitting with for a moment, because it is the number that gives the program's history its specific weight.

Three hundred and sixteen men and one woman dropped into occupied Poland. One hundred and twelve of them did not survive the war — a mortality rate of approximately thirty-five percent, nearly one in three. Of those who died, some were killed in action during partisan operations or resistance activities. Some were captured by the Gestapo and executed. Some died in concentration camps. Some were killed in the Warsaw Uprising of 1944. Some were killed by the Ukrainian nationalist forces operating in the eastern territories. A few died in accidents — the ordinary contingent mortality of warfare that makes no distinction between the extraordinary and the routine.

These numbers are not abstractions. Behind each of the 112 who died is a person who had been in Britain — who had trained in the Scottish Highlands, eaten in RAF mess halls, walked the streets of London, and made the deliberate decision to leave all of that for the darkness over occupied Poland. Each of them had a family. Each had been young enough to have most of their life ahead of them when they made the choice that ended it.

The 204 who survived carried the war with them in ways that lasted the rest of their lives. Many of them, like Elżbieta Zawacka, faced additional persecution in postwar Communist Poland — the AK's wartime service was viewed with deep suspicion by the Soviet-backed government, and former AK members were subject to arrest, imprisonment, and in some cases execution under charges of the same invented variety that killed Witold Pilecki. To have survived the German occupation was not, for many of the Cichociemni, to have reached safety. It was merely to have exchanged one dangerous world for a different one.

What is the right way to understand what the Cichociemni were?

They were soldiers, first and most simply — professional military men who had been trained to the highest standard their program could produce and who served in the most demanding conditions that the war generated. By any military metric — the difficulty of their operational environment, the sophistication of their training, the rate at which they were willing to accept casualties — they belonged among the elite special forces of the Second World War.

They were also something the purely military framing doesn't quite capture. They were people who had gotten out — who had escaped from Poland in 1939 and found their way to Britain, who were by definition among the luckiest of their generation, the ones for whom the series of accidents and decisions and narrow escapes had produced survival rather than capture or death. They were, in the most literal sense, safe. And they chose, voluntarily, to go back.

The reasons were various and individual — patriotism, duty, the specific guilt of the survivor who has escaped what his countrymen have not, the simpler desire to be useful in the most direct possible way. But the choice itself, repeated 317 times by 317 different people who had each arrived at it through their own particular combination of reasons, constitutes something that resists reduction to any single explanation.

They went back because they were Polish, and Poland needed them, and they were the ones who were positioned to answer that need. And one in three of them died for it.

The silent and unseen. They earned the name.

The Boy Who Mapped Peenemünde

Polish Intelligence and the V-Weapons

The first reports were easy to dismiss.

In the intelligence trade, unusual activity is not the same as significant activity. Unusual things happen constantly in wartime — construction projects appear and disappear, military units move without apparent purpose, civilians are displaced from areas that subsequently become restricted zones. The analyst who treats every anomaly as a signal drowns in noise. The skill is in recognizing which anomalies matter, and that recognition requires not just intelligence but judgment — the accumulated intuition of someone who has been reading the landscape long enough to know when something is genuinely different from everything around it.

What was happening on the Baltic coast of occupied Poland in 1942 was genuinely different. It took time for that difference to be recognized, reported, transmitted, and finally understood by the people in London who had the context to make sense of it. The chain of recognition — from the local observers who first noticed that something was wrong to the RAF commanders who acted on what they were told —

ran through some of the most dangerous terrain in occupied Europe and depended at every link on people whose names history has only partially preserved.

At the beginning of that chain was a place called Peenemünde, and at the end of it was a raid that changed the course of the war.

Peenemünde is a narrow peninsula on the island of Usedom, at the mouth of the Oder River where it meets the Baltic Sea — a remote and marshy place that had been, before the war, of no particular significance to anyone. The Germans chose it precisely for its remoteness. In 1936, the Army Weapons Office began construction of a research and development facility on the peninsula that would eventually become the most technologically advanced weapons development complex in the world — the place where Wernher von Braun and his team of rocket engineers were developing the weapons that Hitler believed would change the outcome of the war.

By 1942 Peenemünde was a vast installation. It covered much of the Usedom peninsula, encompassing research laboratories, test stands, production facilities, barracks for thousands of workers, and the infrastructure of a small town constructed for a single purpose. The rockets it was developing — the V-1 flying bomb and the V-2 ballistic missile — were being test-fired with increasing frequency over the Baltic, their trajectories tracked by instruments and their impacts assessed by recovery teams in the impact zones further along the coast.

The German security apparatus around Peenemünde was formidable. The facility was classified at the highest level. Access was strictly controlled. Workers and researchers were subject to comprehensive security screening. The airspace over Usedom was restricted. The local civilian population had been largely displaced from the areas immediately surrounding the installation. Every precaution that the German security services could conceive of had been applied to ensure that what was happening at Peenemünde remained unknown to the Allied intelligence services.

They had not reckoned with the Polish underground.

The intelligence network that eventually produced the Peenemünde picture was not a single organized system directed toward a specific target. It was something more organic and more fragile — a dispersed collection of individual observers, local contacts, and courier links that gathered fragments of information from across the Baltic coast and transmitted them upward through the AK intelligence directorate to the Polish Government-in-Exile in London and from there to British MI6.

The observers were, in many cases, exactly the kind of people that a sophisticated intelligence service might overlook: local Poles living in the areas around the Baltic coast installations, employed in capacities that gave them access to information without making them obvious intelligence targets. Railway workers who noted the frequency and composition of supply trains moving toward the restricted zones. Construction workers and laborers — some of them forced laborers, working in conditions of near-slavery — who observed what was being built and where. Fishermen whose boats took them along coastlines from which the Germans had excluded civilian traffic, who could see from the water what was invisible from the land.

These were not trained intelligence officers. They were ordinary people who understood, with the practical intelligence of those living under occupation, that what they were seeing was significant, and who had the courage — and it was courage, because reporting to the underground in German-occupied Poland was not a safe activity — to pass what they knew to someone who could use it.

The courier links that moved their information upward were maintained by the AK's intelligence directorate — the second bureau, which had developed over the years of the occupation a network of routes and contacts that connected the most remote corners of occupied Poland to the central intelligence apparatus in Warsaw. A report originating with a railway worker near the Baltic coast might pass through three or four couriers before reaching Warsaw, each courier knowing only the person who had given them the material and the person to whom they were delivering it.

The risk at every link in this chain was absolute. A courier arrested with intelligence documents in her possession faced interrogation by the Gestapo — and Gestapo interrogation meant torture, and torture meant that whatever she knew about the chain above and below her was at risk. The system's defense against this was compartmentalization — keeping each link ignorant of everything except the minimum necessary to perform its function — but compartmentalization was a protection, not an immunity. People died maintaining these chains. Some of them died without ever knowing what the fragments of information they were carrying ultimately revealed.

The specific intelligence about Peenemünde began accumulating in the files of the AK's second bureau through 1942, as reports from multiple independent sources in the Baltic coastal region began to paint a consistent picture of unusual activity.

Reports described massive construction on the Usedom peninsula — large concrete structures of a kind that had no obvious civilian purpose, extensive railway infrastructure being laid to service the facility, and a security perimeter that went well beyond what any normal military installation would require. Other reports described strange objects being transported by rail toward the facility — large cylindrical shapes, carefully shrouded, moved at night with security escorts that spoke to their importance.

Then came the sounds and the lights. Local observers along the Baltic coast began reporting, at irregular intervals, what they described as tremendous explosions or thunderclaps from the direction of Usedom, followed by trails of fire visible in the night sky — objects moving with a speed and trajectory that nothing they had previously seen could account for. The reports were consistent across multiple independent sources separated by significant distances, which meant they were almost certainly describing the same phenomenon from different vantage points.

The AK intelligence directorate in Warsaw looked at the accumulating reports and recognized that they were describing something that fell outside the normal categories of military intelligence. This was not a new division being formed or a supply depot being established. Whatever was happening at Peenemünde was different in kind from the ordinary military activity the underground monitored as a matter of course.

The material was transmitted to the Polish Government-in-Exile's intelligence service in London — the Oddział

II, the second department, which maintained the liaison with British intelligence that was the conduit through which Polish intelligence reached Allied hands. The transmission used the courier and wireless routes that connected Warsaw to London — routes that had been developed at enormous cost and that were operated with the meticulous care of a system that understood the consequences of compromise.

In London, the Polish intelligence material arrived at a moment when British scientific intelligence was already beginning to wrestle with evidence of German long-range weapons development from other sources — aerial reconnaissance, signals intelligence, and the reports of agents operating in Germany and the occupied territories. The analyst primarily responsible for assembling this picture was R.V. Jones — the scientific intelligence officer whose work on German weapons systems would later be described by Churchill as having saved countless lives.

Jones had been receiving fragments of evidence about German rocket development since 1939, when an anonymous document — the Oslo Report, delivered to the British embassy in Norway by an unidentified German scientist — had described several advanced German weapons programs including long-range rockets. The Oslo Report had been largely dismissed at the time as too comprehensive to be genuine. By 1942 the accumulation of consistent evidence from multiple independent sources — including the Polish reports — was making dismissal increasingly difficult.

The Polish material was particularly valuable because of its consistency and its specificity. Multiple independent observers, reporting through separate channels, were describing the same facility, the same unusual transports, the same aerial phenomena. The probability that all of them were fabricated or mistaken was vanishingly small. What they were describing was real, and it was at Peenemünde.

The British response was to task photographic reconnaissance aircraft — the high-altitude Spitfires and Mosquitoes of the RAF's photographic reconnaissance units — with systematic coverage of the Usedom peninsula. The photographs they brought back in the spring of 1943 confirmed what the Polish ground intelligence had indicated: a massive facility, concrete test stands of unmistakable purpose, and — in photographs taken in June 1943 — what appeared to be large rocket shapes on the test stands themselves.

The photographic confirmation was provided with crucial assistance from a young woman named Constance Babington Smith, a WAAF photographic interpreter whose eye for anomalous detail in reconnaissance photographs was exceptional. It was Babington Smith who identified the small cruciform shapes on the Peenemünde photographs that turned out to be V-1 flying bombs on their launch ramps — a discovery that added a second weapons system to the target picture and significantly increased the urgency of the British response.

Among the Polish agents whose contribution to the Peenemünde intelligence picture is specifically documented is a young man known in the historical record primarily by his underground alias — a courier and observer whose work in the Baltic coastal region produced some of the earliest and most specific reports about the Usedom facility. His story illustrates both what the intelligence chain required of the individuals who maintained it and what it cost them.

He was, by the accounts that have survived, barely out of his teens — a student before the occupation, recruited into the AK network through the connections of family or friends or neighborhood, the ordinary paths by which the underground grew its membership. His assignment to the Baltic coastal region placed him in one of the more exposed positions in the entire AK intelligence network — an area where the German security presence was heavy, where the local Polish population was under particular pressure, and where the work he was doing put him in proximity to one of Germany's most sensitive secrets.

He moved through the restricted zones around Peenemünde using cover identities and the practiced invisibility of someone who had learned, through necessity and training, how to be where he should not be without appearing to be anything other than exactly where he belonged. He observed. He sketched — rough maps and diagrams of what he could see from available vantage points, the locations of structures and launch facilities and railway connections, the patterns of activity that told a trained observer what a facility was for even when its official designation revealed nothing.

His sketches and reports made their way south through the courier chain, through Warsaw, through the Government-in-Exile's intelligence channels, and eventually to London. Whether he ever knew what became of the intelligence he risked his life to gather — whether he survived the war long enough to learn about Operation Hydra and its consequences — the historical record does not clearly establish.

He was one of many. The intelligence picture that drove the Peenemünde decision was built from dozens of contributions like his — individual fragments that meant little in isolation and everything in combination.

Operation Hydra — the RAF bombing raid on Peenemünde — was executed on the night of August 17 to 18, 1943. It was one of the largest and most precisely planned bombing operations the RAF had conducted to that point in the war: nearly 600 heavy bombers, flying in multiple waves, targeting the research facilities, the production shops, the scientists' housing estate, and the forced labor camp that housed the concentration camp prisoners who provided much of Peenemünde's workforce.

The raid was conducted under conditions of considerable risk. Peenemünde was at the extreme range of Bomber Command's operational radius from its bases in England. The flight north over the North Sea and then east along the Baltic coast was long and exposed. The German night fighter response, once the raid's target became clear, was fierce — 40 RAF aircraft were shot down, and 243 aircrew were killed. Among the dead were a disproportionate number of experienced crews, lost at a moment in the air war when experienced crews were among Bomber Command's most valuable assets.

The damage inflicted on Peenemünde was significant. The production facilities were heavily damaged. The scientists' housing estate — targeted specifically because the research program depended on the concentration of irreplaceable scientific expertise — was destroyed, killing a number of senior engineers and scientists. Among the dead was Dr. Walter Thiel, the V-2's chief propulsion engineer — a loss that the German rocket program felt acutely in the months that followed.

The strategic assessment of Operation Hydra's impact is necessarily somewhat speculative — precise timelines for weapons programs that were not completed on schedule are difficult to reconstruct with confidence. The consensus among historians who have examined the German rocket program's records is that the Peenemünde raid delayed the operational deployment of the V-2 by approximately four to six months.

Four to six months. It is worth dwelling on what that delay meant in concrete human terms.

The V-2 bombardment of Britain and the occupied territories began in September 1944. Working backward from the raid's estimated delay, an unimpeded V-2 program might have begun its operational campaign in the spring of 1944 — before the Normandy landings, at a moment when the Allied war effort was building toward its most critical operation and when the political and psychological impact of a sustained ballistic missile campaign against London might have been significantly greater than what actually occurred.

The V-2 as deployed killed approximately 9,000 people — a horrific number, though smaller than Hitler had hoped and smaller than the weapon's advocates had promised. Whether an earlier and potentially larger-scale V-2 campaign against a pre-invasion Britain would have killed more, or disrupted the Overlord planning, or produced political pressure for negotiation that a post-Normandy Britain was better positioned to resist — these are counterfactuals that cannot be resolved with certainty. What can be said is that the delay mattered, and that the delay was in significant part the product of intelligence that began with Polish observers on the Baltic coast noting that something unusual was happening on the Usedom peninsula.

The Polish contribution to the Allied understanding of the V-weapons program extended beyond the Peenemünde intelligence. Throughout 1943 and 1944, as the Germans developed and deployed the V-1 launch infrastructure across occupied northern France and the Low Countries, AK-connected intelligence networks provided detailed reports on construction sites, launch ramp locations, and supply arrangements that informed the Allied bombing campaign against the V-weapon infrastructure.

The chain that ran from a young courier sketching rough maps near the Baltic coast to the RAF's target planning rooms in High Wycombe was not a direct one. It ran through Warsaw and through London, through the Polish Government-in-Exile's intelligence service and through the files of British MI6, through the analytical work of R.V. Jones and his colleagues and through the photographic interpreters who confirmed what the ground intelligence had indicated. At every point it depended on people doing their jobs with precision and courage — and on the particular courage of the people at the beginning of the chain, the ones who gathered the raw intelligence in the most dangerous conditions, who had no way of knowing whether what they were risking their lives for was reaching anyone who could use it.

It was. The intelligence reached its destination. The raid happened. The delay was real. The connection between the Polish observers on the Baltic coast and the bombs that fell on Peenemünde on the night of August 17, 1943 is not direct in the way that a single agent's report producing a single military action is direct — intelligence work is rarely that clean. But it is real, and it is documented, and it deserves to be part of the history of what the Polish underground accomplished in the years when it was fighting a war that most of the world could not see.

The silent work of invisible people, producing consequences that echoed across the entire arc of the war.

That, in the end, is what intelligence is.

INDEPENDENT STATE OF CROATIA
GERMAN-OCCUPIED SERBIA
ZAGREB
Sava River
BELGRADE
DINARIC ALPS
BOSNIAN HIGHLANDS
DRVAR
ADRIATIC SEA
Neretva River
ITALIAN-OCCUPIED
Vis
SARAJEVO
ITALIAN-OCCUPIED
N
W
E
S
YUGOSLAVIA
1941 – 1945
0 50 100 150 200 200
Miles

The Mountain Republic

How Tito Built an Army from Rubble

Yugoslavia died in eleven days.

The German invasion that began on April 6, 1941 — launched without formal declaration of war, opened with a bombing raid on Belgrade that killed thousands of civilians in the first hours — encountered a Yugoslav army that was undermined by ethnic divisions, inadequate equipment, and a command structure that had never been designed to fight the kind of war that the Wehrmacht had spent two years perfecting against the best armies in Europe. By April 17, the Yugoslav government had surrendered and its king had fled into exile. The country that had existed since 1918 — a complicated, fractious, multiethnic state that had never fully resolved the tensions between its constituent peoples — had ceased to exist as a political entity.

What replaced it was a patchwork of occupation and puppet administration that satisfied none of its architects and tormented virtually everyone who lived within it. Germany took the northern slice of Slovenia and occupied Serbia directly. Italy absorbed the Adriatic coast and established a sphere of influence over Montenegro. Hungary took back territories it had lost after the First World War. Bulgaria did the same in Macedonia. And in the ruins of what had been Croatia and Bosnia-Herzegovina, the Germans and Italians installed a puppet state — the Independent State of Croatia, the NDH — under the leadership of the Ustaše movement, a Croatian fascist organization whose ideology of ethnic nationalism expressed itself almost immediately in a campaign of mass murder against the Serb, Jewish, and Roma populations within its borders.

Into this landscape of violence and fragmentation, in the summer of 1941, walked Josip Broz Tito — and began building an army.

Josip Broz had been many things before he became Tito. He had been a metalworker, a prisoner of war in Russia during the First World War, a Communist organizer who had spent years moving through the underground networks of European Communism under a succession of aliases, and a veteran of the Spanish Civil War. He was forty-nine years old in 1941 — older than most resistance leaders, shaped by a harder and more various life than most of them had lived, and possessed of a quality that his biography had been, in some sense, custom-designed to produce: the ability to operate effectively in conditions of extreme danger, uncertainty, and organizational chaos.

He was also, it must be said from the outset, ruthless in ways that his postwar mythology tended to obscure. Tito's Yugoslavia became, after the war, a Communist state — less brutal than Stalin's Soviet Union but not a democracy by any meaningful standard — and the man who built the Partisan movement was the same man who built that state, with all that implies about his methods and his priorities. The courage and organizational genius that made him an extraordinary resistance leader were inseparable from a political intelligence that was always calculating the postwar landscape even while fighting the current war. Understanding Tito requires holding both of these things simultaneously — the genuine greatness and the genuine ruthlessness — without allowing either to crowd out the other.

The moment that set everything in motion came on June 22, 1941 — the day Germany invaded the Soviet Union. Until that moment, the Yugoslav Communist Party had been operating under the constraints of the Molotov-Ribbentrop Pact — the non-aggression agreement between Germany and the Soviet Union that had made open Communist resistance to German occupation politically complicated. The moment Germany attacked the Soviet Union, those constraints dissolved. Stalin's Comintern ordered Communist parties across occupied Europe to begin active resistance. Tito was already thinking ahead of the instruction.

On July 4, 1941 — a date that would be celebrated as a national holiday in Tito's Yugoslavia — the Central Committee of the Yugoslav Communist Party met in Belgrade and voted to launch armed resistance against the occupation. Tito had been preparing for this moment since April. He had maps. He had plans. He had, in embryo, the organizational structure of the movement he intended to build.

He had, at that moment, approximately 12,000 party members across Yugoslavia — most of them civilians with no military training, organized into cells that had been designed for underground political work rather than armed resistance. It was not much. It was what he had.

He went to work.

The first Partisan operations in the summer and autumn of 1941 were conducted primarily in Serbia — ambushes of German vehicles, attacks on collaborationist police posts, sabotage of railway lines and communication infrastructure. They were small in scale and large in consequence, because the German response to them established immediately the terms on which the resistance war in Yugoslavia would be fought.

On September 16, 1941, the German military commander in Serbia issued an order that made explicit what had previously been implied: for every German soldier killed by resistance action, 100 Serbian civilians would be executed in reprisal. For every German soldier wounded, 50 would be shot. The order was not empty. On October 21, 1941, in the town of Kragujevac, German troops rounded up the male population of the town and surrounding villages — including schoolboys who had been taken directly from their classrooms — and shot 2,778 people in a single day. The Kragujevac massacre was a reprisal for a Partisan ambush that had killed 10 German soldiers and wounded 26.

The arithmetic was not abstract. It was written in the bodies of 2,778 people who had nothing to do with the ambush that killed them.

This was the fundamental moral crisis of Yugoslav resistance — a crisis more acute than anything faced by the resistance movements of France or Poland, because nowhere else in occupied Europe was the reprisal ratio so high, so consistently applied, and so massively documented. Every Partisan operation that killed German soldiers would be paid for by civilians. The calculation that the French Resistance had faced at Tulle and Oradour-sur-Glane — the unbearable arithmetic of resistance — was in Yugoslavia not an occasional horror but a standing operational reality.

Tito's response to this crisis was characteristically complex. He did not stop fighting. He was constitutionally incapable of stopping, and he understood — correctly, in the judgment of history — that a resistance that stopped fighting when the reprisals became too costly had been defeated as surely as one that was destroyed in the field. But he also understood that the reprisal policy was a strategic weapon the Germans were deploying against him — designed not just to punish resistance but to turn the civilian population against the Partisans, to make the cost of sheltering or supporting them too high for ordinary people to bear.

His response was to make the Partisans worth supporting.

The organizational principles that Tito imposed on the Partisan movement from its earliest days were as important as any military operation the Partisans conducted, and they distinguished the movement from virtually every other resistance organization in occupied Europe.

Discipline was absolute and its enforcement was not gentle. Tito issued orders early in the movement's development that were unambiguous: Partisan fighters did not steal from the civilian population. They did not loot. They did not commit atrocities against civilians — not Serbian civilians, not Croatian civilians, not Muslim civilians, not any civilian regardless of their ethnicity or their perceived relationship to the various factions of the Yugoslav civil war that was running alongside and intertwined with the resistance against the occupation. A Partisan who violated these orders faced a tribunal. Violations serious enough — and theft and murder were both serious enough — faced execution.

This was not sentimentality. It was strategy of the highest order. Tito understood that the Partisans' only sustainable source of supply, intelligence, shelter, and recruitment was the civilian population. A movement that preyed on the population it claimed to protect would eventually be destroyed by that population's withdrawal of support — if not by active denunciation, then by the simple refusal to feed, shelter, and warn fighters who had made themselves indistinguishable from another form of banditry. The Partisans needed the people. The people needed to believe that the Partisans were worth the risk.

This calculation set the Partisans apart from their primary rivals in the Yugoslav resistance — the Chetniks, the Serbian royalist movement led by General Dragoljub Mihailović. The Chetniks had begun the resistance with motivations as patriotic as the Partisans', but their approach to the reprisal problem had led them in a different direction. Mihailović concluded early that large-scale military operations against the Germans were not worth the civilian cost, and gradually moved toward a policy of waiting — preserving his forces for the moment of liberation rather than fighting actively in the present. In practice this policy shaded, in some Chetnik units, into collaboration with the Italian occupation forces and eventually with the Germans — not collaboration in the ideological sense, but tactical cooperation that the Partisans were not slow to exploit politically.

The political structure that Tito built alongside the military one was, in its ambition and its execution, as remarkable as the army itself.

From the beginning, Tito conceived of the Partisan movement as more than a military organization. It was a government in waiting — or more precisely, a government in motion, already exercising the functions of administration in the territories it controlled even before liberation was a realistic prospect. The Partisans established liberated zones — areas cleared of German and Italian forces where Partisan administration replaced occupation authority — and in these zones they created the institutional structures that would eventually become the government of postwar Yugoslavia.

People's Liberation Committees were established in liberated villages and districts — administrative bodies that managed local governance, taxation, and the provision of services. Courts were organized. Schools were opened. A Partisan press produced newspapers and pamphlets. The movement recruited not just fighters but administrators, doctors, teachers, journalists — the full range of human capacity that a functioning society requires.

This was Tito's most significant strategic insight, and it distinguished the Yugoslav Partisans from every other resistance movement of the war: that the liberation struggle and the building of the postwar state were not separate projects to be pursued sequentially, but a single project to be pursued simultaneously. The Partisans were not fighting to restore Yugoslavia to what it had been before April 1941. They were fighting to create something that had never existed — a Yugoslavia in which the ethnic tensions that had plagued the interwar state would be resolved, not by the dominance of one group over the others, but by a new political framework that transcended ethnic identity.

Whether that vision was ultimately realized, and at what cost, belongs to a history that extends well beyond the war. What matters here is that the vision was genuine, that it was communicated to the fighters who were risking their lives for it, and that it gave the Partisan movement a political coherence and a forward momentum that purely military resistance organizations lacked.

The Germans recognized the threat the Partisans represented and responded with the full weight of their occupation machinery.

The First Offensive — the German military operation designed to destroy the Partisan movement in Serbia in the autumn of 1941 — was conducted with the coordinated deployment of multiple Wehrmacht divisions supported by collaboration forces. It succeeded in clearing the Partisans from Serbia itself, forcing Tito and his main force out of the territory where they had been operating and into the mountains of Bosnia — a tactical defeat that was, from the perspective of what followed, also a strategic liberation. The Bosnian mountains were terrain where the Partisans' advantages — mobility, local knowledge, the support of a population with long traditions of resistance to outside authority — could be exploited more fully than in the accessible lowlands of Serbia.

The Second Offensive, conducted in January 1942, attempted to pursue and destroy the Partisan force in its new operational area. It failed. The Partisans moved faster than the German forces pursuing them, used the terrain with a skill that reflected both their commanders' military education and their fighters' intimate knowledge of the landscape, and emerged from the offensive bloodied but intact — and larger than when it began. Recruitment continued even as the German pursuit was underway. Men who had watched the German reprisal killings in their villages and who had concluded that the risk of fighting was not materially greater than the risk of not fighting came to the Partisans in the mountains.

By the end of 1942, Tito commanded a force of approximately 150,000 fighters organized into divisions and corps — a military formation of conventional scale, not a guerrilla band. It was supplied primarily by what it captured from the enemy and by what it could extract from the territories it controlled, supplemented by a supply operation from Allied sources that was still, at this point, limited and unreliable.

Tito himself, through all of this, was a presence that his fighters experienced as both physically immediate and strategically remote — a commander who was often at the front, who shared the conditions of his soldiers with a consistency that built genuine loyalty, and who was simultaneously always thinking several moves ahead in a game that extended far beyond the current battle.

He was not an easy man. His charm — and he had considerable charm, the kind that comes from genuine interest in the people around him rather than from performance — coexisted with a capacity for hard decision that did not flinch from the human cost of what he was doing. He ordered executions. He made decisions that sent people to their deaths in operations whose success was not certain and whose failure would be permanent. He did all of this with the equanimity of a man who had decided, at some fundamental level, that the alternative — not deciding, not fighting, not paying the cost — was worse.

He was also, and this is important for understanding the movement he built, a Yugoslav in a way that few of his contemporaries managed to be. In a country being torn apart by ethnic violence — the Ustaše killing Serbs, Chetniks killing Croats and Muslims, everyone killing Jews — Tito insisted on a Partisan movement that was ethnically mixed, that recruited across all of Yugoslavia's communities, and that treated ethnic nationalism as an enemy as dangerous as the German occupation. His own background — he was Croatian by birth, had a Slovenian mother, had spent years in international Communist networks — may have made this easier for him to sustain than it would have been for a man whose identity was more narrowly ethnic. Whatever its source, it was one of his most important contributions to what the Partisans became.

By 1944 the force that had numbered a few hundred fighters in the summer of 1941 had grown to approximately 800,000 — the largest resistance army in occupied Europe, controlling significant portions of Yugoslav territory, receiving substantial Allied supply, and conducting military operations of a scale and sophistication that bore no resemblance to the guerrilla skirmishing of three years earlier.

The journey from those first ambushes in Serbian summer to the army of 1944 had cost, by the most conservative estimates, approximately one million Yugoslav lives — fighters, civilians killed in reprisals, victims of the Ustaše's ethnic killing program, and casualties of the civil war between Partisans and Chetniks that ran alongside the resistance war against the occupiers. It is a number that demands to be held alongside the military achievement — not to diminish the achievement, but to give it the moral weight it actually carried.

Tito had built his army from rubble. The rubble had been people.

That is the fact that his postwar mythology preferred to soften and that honest history cannot allow to be softened. The Yugoslavia that emerged from the war was shaped by the Partisan movement — its institutions, its ideology, its ethnic framework, its political culture. It was also shaped by the million dead, and by the choices that were made along the way about whose deaths were acceptable and whose were not.

Tito was a great man in the particular sense that history reserves for people who accomplish things of genuine historical magnitude. He was also a man whose greatness was inseparable from his ruthlessness, and whose monument was built on foundations that included the bodies of people who had not chosen to be part of his project.

Both of these things are true. Neither cancels the other.

The mountain republic he built endured for decades after the war that created it. Like most things built in conditions of extreme violence and extreme necessity, it contained within it the seeds of what would eventually destroy it. But that story belongs to a different book.

This one is about how it was built — and what it cost.

Operation Rösselsprung

The Hunt for Tito

The Germans had been trying to kill Josip Broz Tito for three years.

They had launched five major offensives against the Partisan movement he commanded — operations involving tens of thousands of troops, coordinated air support, and the full weight of the German military machine in the Balkans. Each offensive had failed to achieve its primary objective. The Partisans had been pushed, battered, forced to retreat across mountains and rivers in conditions that killed thousands of fighters. But Tito had survived, the movement had survived, and each time the Germans withdrew from their latest offensive the Partisans had reconstituted, recruited, and grown stronger than before.

By the spring of 1944 the German military command in the Balkans had reached a conclusion that conventional military operations alone would not reach: that Tito himself was the irreplaceable center of the Partisan movement, and that destroying the movement required first destroying the man. The offensives had failed to catch him because he was always moving, always a step ahead of the German advance, surrounded by a security apparatus that had been refined through three years of operating in conditions where discovery meant death.

What was needed was something different. Something faster. Something that could reach past the Partisan security perimeter and put German soldiers in the same room as Tito before anyone knew they were coming.

What was needed, the planners concluded, was an airborne assault.

The intelligence work that made Operation Rösselsprung possible had been accumulating for months, built from a combination of aerial reconnaissance, signals intelligence, and the reports of agents and informers operating within or around the Partisan-controlled areas of Bosnia.

By early 1944 German intelligence had established, with reasonable confidence, that Tito's main headquarters was located in the town of Drvar — a small timber-industry town in the mountains of western Bosnia, in territory the Partisans had been controlling for months and had fortified accordingly. More specifically, intelligence indicated that Tito himself was using a cave in the cliff face above the town as his personal headquarters — a natural feature that provided both physical protection and concealment from aerial observation.

The cave was real. Tito had been using it since February 1944 — a large natural cavity in the limestone cliff above Drvar that had been fitted out with the basic infrastructure of a military headquarters: communications equipment, maps, a sleeping area, the minimum necessary to sustain the command functions that Tito performed from it. It was secure against conventional ground attack — the approaches to it were controlled by Partisan security units, and any ground force attempting to reach it would have to fight its way through the town and up the cliff face under fire. It was not secure against soldiers landing on top of it.

The planning for Operation Rösselsprung — Knight's Move, the chess term for the piece that jumps over obstacles to reach its target — was conducted at the headquarters of Army Group F under the overall direction of Field Marshal Maximilian von Weichs, with operational planning delegated to the commanders of the forces that would execute it. The concept was a combined arms operation: a parachute and glider assault directly on and around Drvar, landing troops inside the Partisan security perimeter before a response could be organized, followed by a converging ground assault from multiple directions to close off Tito's escape routes.

The assault force was the 500th SS Parachute Battalion — a unit that had been formed specifically for special operations of this kind, composed of volunteers drawn from across the SS and trained in parachute and glider insertion techniques. The battalion numbered approximately 874 men — not a large force by conventional military standards, but sufficient, the planners calculated, to overwhelm the Partisan security detachments in Drvar long enough for the ground forces to close the net.

The date chosen for the operation was May 25, 1944.

It was Tito's fifty-second birthday.

The morning of May 25, 1944 began in Drvar with the particular clarity of a Bosnian mountain spring — cool air, long shadows from the surrounding ridges, the town going about its business with the careful normalcy of a place that had learned to maintain routines in the presence of war.

Tito was in his cave above the town. The Allied military missions attached to his headquarters — British, American, and Soviet liaison officers whose presence reflected the degree to which the Partisans had become a recognized Allied force — were in their billets in and around the town. The Partisan security detachments were at their posts. Scouts on the surrounding ridges were watching the approaches.

None of them were watching the sky.

At approximately 0700, the first wave of German aircraft appeared over Drvar — Junkers Ju 52 transport aircraft and DFS 230 gliders, coming in low and fast from the direction the Partisan lookouts had least expected. The parachutists of the first wave began dropping almost simultaneously with the gliders landing — some of them touching down in the town itself, others on the open ground around it, a specific glider assault group landing directly in front of the cliff face below Tito's cave.

The surprise was not complete — the Partisan security detachments responded faster than the German planners had anticipated, and the fighting that erupted within minutes of the first landings was immediate and savage. But the shock of the assault, the noise and confusion of parachutists dropping and gliders crash-landing in a small town that had never experienced a direct airborne attack, bought the German assault teams the minutes they needed to begin moving toward their objectives.

The group assigned to the cave — the element of the operation most critical to its success — landed as close to the cliff face as the terrain allowed and began moving toward the entrance. They were moving uphill, under fire from Partisan defenders who had positioned themselves on the cliff above and around the cave entrance, but they were moving. For a period that the postwar accounts place at somewhere between twenty and forty minutes — a period of extraordinary confusion in which the outcome of the entire operation was genuinely in balance — they were close enough to Tito's position that the difference between capture and escape was being measured in meters and minutes.

Inside the cave, the first awareness of what was happening came from the sound — the unmistakable engine noise of aircraft at low altitude, followed almost immediately by the sounds of fighting in the town below. Tito's security detail reacted with the professionalism of people who had been preparing for exactly this kind of emergency without knowing when it would come.

The cave had a rear exit — a tunnel that connected the main chamber to a point higher on the cliff face, above and behind the German assault group that was fighting its way toward the cave entrance. The decision to use it was made quickly. Tito, in the accounts that have survived from multiple participants, was not a man who needed to be persuaded to move — he understood immediately what the assault represented and what his capture or death would mean for everything he had built.

He left through the rear tunnel. With him went members of his personal staff, his security detail, and — in an detail that has become one of the more celebrated small facts of the entire operation — his dog, a German Shepherd named Tigar, who was reportedly lowered down the cliff face on a rope when the descent proved too steep for the dog to manage unassisted.

The escape route took them up and over the cliff face above the cave, into the forest on the reverse slope, and away from

Drvar in the direction that the German ground forces had not yet closed. It was, by any measure, a close thing. The German assault group reached the cave entrance and entered the main chamber within minutes of Tito's departure through the rear tunnel. They found his uniform — he had not had time to dress fully — his military cap, his medals, and a half-finished birthday cake that had been prepared for the occasion.

They did not find Tito.

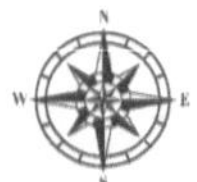

The hours that followed the initial assault were a desperate running fight across the mountains above Drvar, as Tito and his group moved on foot through terrain that was simultaneously their best protection and their greatest physical challenge, while the German ground forces that had been positioned to close the encirclement moved to cut off the escape routes.

The Partisan security detachments in and around Drvar fought with a ferocity that slowed the German consolidation of the town and bought time for Tito's group to extend its lead. Individual Partisan units — some of them barely trained recruits who had been in the movement for weeks rather than months — held positions against German forces many times their strength, understanding that the time they purchased with their resistance was time Tito was using to get further away.

The Allied liaison officers attached to Tito's headquarters were caught up in the chaos of the initial assault. Fitzroy Maclean — the British officer whose role in the Allied-Partisan relationship will be examined in the following chapter

— was not present at Drvar on the day of the assault, having left the headquarters shortly before. Other members of the British mission were present and participated in the fighting retreat, an experience that provided the Allied governments with a more vivid understanding of what the Partisans were living through than any intelligence report had managed to convey.

The German ground forces converging on Drvar from multiple directions were substantially stronger than the airborne force that had opened the operation, but they faced the same problem that every German offensive against the Partisans had faced: the Partisans moved faster in their own mountains than German formations could follow. The encirclement that was supposed to close around Drvar never fully closed — gaps existed in the German cordon, and Tito's group found them.

Tito and his group reached the railway town of Potoci, east of Drvar, after a march of several days through the mountains. From Potoci, communications with Allied headquarters allowed the organization of what came next — an evacuation that reflected, in its complexity and its ultimate success, exactly how important the Allied high command had concluded Tito was to the war effort in the Balkans.

The first evacuation was by Soviet aircraft — a Douglas C-47 dispatched from the Soviet mission, which landed at a makeshift airstrip near Potoci and flew Tito to the Italian city of Bari, where Allied Forces Headquarters in Italy was located. From Bari, after consultations with Allied commanders that addressed both the immediate military situation and the longer-term question of where Tito could most effectively command the Partisan forces, he was transferred to the island of Vis — a small Adriatic island that had been turned into an Allied military base and that offered, for the first time in Tito's wartime career, a headquarters that was physically secure from German attack.

The British destroyer that carried him to Vis was HMS Blackmore. When he came ashore on the island, he was greeted by British officers who had been told that their principal duty was to ensure that Josip Broz Tito did not die on Allied-controlled territory after having survived three years of German attempts to kill him in his own.

He remained on Vis for several weeks, commanding the Partisan forces by wireless while the German offensive that had followed the Drvar assault ran its course. The Partisans, without Tito present to be captured, continued to function — a demonstration of the organizational depth that three years of movement-building had produced. The German ground offensive achieved significant local successes, inflicting casualties and capturing territory. It did not destroy the Partisan movement, because the Partisan movement was no longer something that could be destroyed by killing or capturing any single person, even its commander.

Except that it could have been, in May 1944, more than at any other point in the previous three years. That is the most important thing about Operation Rösselsprung.

The question of what Tito's capture or death at Drvar would have meant for the war is a counterfactual that cannot be resolved with certainty, but it can be examined with some precision.

By May 1944 the Partisan movement was large enough — 800,000 fighters, significant liberated territory, an established political structure — that it would not have simply collapsed in the absence of its leader. The organizational depth that Tito had built was real. There were competent commanders at every level who could have continued operations. The movement had momentum, popular support, and Allied supply that would not have been withdrawn simply because its commander was gone.

But Tito was more than a military commander. He was the political center of the Partisan project — the figure whose authority transcended the ethnic and ideological tensions within the movement, whose relationships with Allied governments were personal as well as institutional, and whose vision of what postwar Yugoslavia would be provided the movement with the political coherence that its military operations required. There was no obvious successor who combined his military authority with his political stature.

The Allied assessment, communicated clearly in the priority given to his evacuation, was that his capture or death would have damaged the Yugoslav resistance in ways that went beyond military command. It would have created a succession crisis within the movement at the moment when the war in the Balkans was approaching its decisive phase. It would have complicated the Allied relationship with the Yugoslav resistance at a moment when the coordination of Partisan operations with the broader Allied strategic picture was becoming increasingly important. And it would have provided the Germans with a propaganda victory of significant value — the capture or killing of the most celebrated resistance leader in occupied Europe.

The glider assault group that reached Tito's cave within minutes of his departure through the rear tunnel came closer to all of those consequences than any German operation before or since.

The 500th SS Parachute Battalion suffered severe casualties in the fighting at Drvar and the subsequent German ground operations. The battalion had gone into the operation as an elite unit. It came out of it depleted and combat-ineffective, requiring substantial time to reconstitute. Of the 874 men who jumped or landed by glider on May 25, 1944, approximately 576 became casualties — killed, wounded, or captured. It was a casualty rate of over sixty percent for an operation that had failed to achieve its primary objective.

The German ground forces that followed up the airborne assault achieved tactical successes — they captured territory, killed Partisan fighters, and forced the main Partisan forces in the Drvar area to withdraw. But tactical success without the capture or killing of Tito was not what Operation Rösselsprung had been designed to achieve. By the metric of its own stated objective, the operation had failed.

The man it had been designed to kill was on an Adriatic island, planning his return.

Tito returned to Yugoslav soil in September 1944, slipping covertly from Vis to the liberated areas of eastern Yugoslavia as Soviet forces advancing from the east and Partisan forces advancing from within the country converged on Belgrade. By October 1944, the Yugoslav capital was liberated — the first Axis-occupied European capital to be freed by a combination of resistance forces and Allied armies, a fact that Tito's postwar government would not allow anyone to forget.

Operation Rösselsprung entered the historical record as one of the more audacious special operations of the Second World War — a bold concept, competently executed, that failed by the narrowest of margins to achieve an objective that might, had it succeeded, have changed the course of the war in the Balkans. The margin of failure was a rear tunnel and the twenty minutes between when the assault group landed and when it reached the cave entrance.

Twenty minutes. A tunnel. A dog lowered down a cliff on a rope.

The things that turn the hinge of history are rarely as large as the histories built around them suggest. Sometimes they are exactly this small.

The Man Churchill Sent

Fitzroy Maclean and the SOE Mission

Fitzroy Maclean was thirty-two years old when he parachuted into occupied Yugoslavia, and he had already lived more lives than most people manage in a full span of years.

He had been a diplomat — a Foreign Office man who had served in Moscow in the 1930s, watching Stalin's show trials from a seat close enough to see the faces of the accused, and who had traveled through Soviet Central Asia in defiance of explicit official prohibition, filing dispatches that read like adventure fiction because the adventures were real. He had been a soldier — a member of the SAS in North Africa, conducting raids behind German lines with the particular combination of physical courage and intellectual detachment that the best special forces officers cultivate. He had been, briefly, a Member of Parliament — elected in 1941 in a by-election that he had contested partly, by his own later admission, as a way of escaping the Foreign Office's grip on his career and getting himself to the war.

He was, in the language that the British ruling class used to describe its own when it meant the highest possible compliment, a remarkable man. Churchill, who was himself a remarkable man and therefore a reliable judge of the quality in others, recognized it immediately.

In the summer of 1943, Churchill summoned Maclean and gave him a mission that combined the military and the political in proportions that only Churchill could have conceived: parachute into Yugoslavia, find Tito, assess the Partisan movement's military effectiveness, and report back with a recommendation on whether Britain should shift its support from Mihailović's Chetniks — who were receiving British supply and had a British liaison mission attached to them — to the Partisans.

The decision that would flow from that recommendation would shape the postwar history of the Balkans.

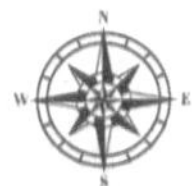

To understand what Maclean was being sent to assess, it is necessary to understand the state of British knowledge about Yugoslavia in the summer of 1943 — which is to say, the state of profound uncertainty that had prevailed since the beginning of the occupation.

Britain had been supporting Mihailović since 1941 — the Serbian general who had remained in Yugoslavia after the April collapse, taken to the mountains with a group of officers and men, and established the Chetnik movement as what the British hoped would be the nucleus of a serious resistance force. Mihailović had been promoted, decorated, and appointed Minister of War by the Yugoslav government in exile. BBC broadcasts had celebrated him as a hero. The British government had invested considerable political capital in the proposition that he was the primary and legitimate representative of Yugoslav resistance.

The problem was that the intelligence reaching London from inside Yugoslavia was increasingly inconsistent with that proposition. Reports from SOE agents and from signal intercepts suggested that Mihailović's forces were not conducting the kind of active resistance operations that would justify the support they were receiving. More troublingly, some reports suggested active cooperation between Chetnik units and Italian — and in some cases German — forces against the Partisans.

At the same time, reports about the Partisans — who had been receiving no British support — described a militarily active force of growing size and effectiveness that was tying down significant German and Italian forces across Yugoslavia. The operational calculus was becoming difficult to ignore: if the goal was to keep Axis forces occupied in Yugoslavia and away from other theaters where British forces were fighting, which movement was actually achieving that goal?

The answer, the intelligence increasingly suggested, was Tito's Partisans.

Churchill needed someone he trusted to go in and settle the question. He chose Maclean.

Maclean arrived in Yugoslavia on the night of September 17, 1943, parachuting from a Halifax bomber into the darkness above the mountains of Bosnia. The drop was, by the standards of wartime parachute insertions, reasonably successful — Maclean landed in the correct general area, made contact with the Partisan reception committee that had been organized to meet him, and was taken to meet Tito within days of his arrival.

His first impression of Tito was one that he would refine over the months that followed but never substantially revise: a man of considerable physical presence, obvious intelligence, and a quality of controlled authority that was the product not of rank or title but of personality and demonstrated competence. Tito had been leading this movement for two years under conditions that would have broken most people. The fact that he was still here, still commanding, still expanding the force under his control, was itself a form of evidence that Maclean found more persuasive than any briefing document.

The assessment that Maclean conducted over the following weeks was not conducted from a safe distance. He traveled with Partisan units, observed their operations, examined their organization, and subjected himself to the same physical conditions — the mountain marches, the inadequate food, the constant German pressure — that the fighters under Tito's command were living with every day. This was deliberate. He understood that an assessment conducted from a comfortable headquarters would tell him what the Partisans wanted him to know. An assessment conducted on the march would tell him what they actually were.

What he found was a military force of genuine effectiveness — larger, better organized, and more actively engaged with the enemy than any British assessment had suggested. The Partisans were not a guerrilla band. They were a conventional military organization of divisional and corps structure, capable of holding territory against German attacks and of conducting offensive operations that produced measurable results. The intelligence about their size — estimates that had seemed inflated in London — proved, on direct observation, to be conservative rather than exaggerated.

He also found evidence of the Chetnik collaboration with Axis forces that the signal intercepts had suggested. Not uniformly — the Chetnik situation was more complex than a simple collaboration verdict would suggest, with different formations behaving differently in different areas — but sufficiently consistent, and sufficiently documented in captured Italian and German records that Partisan intelligence officers showed him, to be impossible to dismiss as Partisan propaganda.

The SOE mission that Maclean commanded in Yugoslavia grew steadily after his arrival, as the scale of the Partisan operation and the volume of coordination required both expanded. Teams of British officers and NCOs were inserted throughout the Partisan-controlled areas of Yugoslavia, each team responsible for liaison with local Partisan commanders, coordination of supply drops, and communication with London and Cairo.

The work these teams did was unglamorous in its daily texture and critical in its operational impact. A supply drop to a Partisan formation required the team to communicate the unit's location and needs to headquarters, receive confirmation of an incoming drop, organize a reception committee, signal the incoming aircraft with fires or torches in the designated pattern, and then manage the distribution of whatever arrived — weapons, ammunition, medical supplies, explosives — among units that were chronically short of everything and that had commanders with strong opinions about the appropriate allocation of scarce resources.

The radio communications that sustained these operations were conducted under conditions that any peacetime signals officer would have considered impossible. Wireless sets powered by hand-cranked generators, operated from positions that changed constantly as the Partisan formations moved, transmitting in encoded bursts through the mountain terrain that created unpredictable effects on signal propagation — these were the tools with which the mission maintained its link to the Allied world.

The operators who worked these sets were among the most valuable people in the mission, and they were treated accordingly. An SOE team that lost its wireless operator to German fire or to the physical attrition of mountain campaigning had lost its primary function. Operators were protected with a degree of care that the team commanders were sometimes accused of taking to excess — the accusation invariably made by people who did not fully appreciate how completely the team's usefulness depended on maintaining that radio link.

The personal relationships that developed between SOE mission members and the Partisan officers they worked alongside were, in many cases, as important to the mission's operational effectiveness as any formal coordination mechanism. Partisan commanders who trusted their British liaison officers shared intelligence, consulted on operational planning, and coordinated their activities with Allied requests in ways that went beyond what formal liaison protocols could have achieved.

The trust was not given automatically and was not maintained without effort. British officers who treated Partisan commanders with the condescension of representatives of a great power dealing with irregular fighters quickly found that the Partisans had well-developed antennae for exactly that kind of attitude and responded to it by sharing as little as possible. British officers who demonstrated genuine respect for what the Partisans had accomplished — who understood that the movement had been fighting and surviving for two years before any British officer parachuted in to help — found a different kind of reception.

Maclean himself set the tone. His natural instinct, shaped by his diplomatic background and his genuine intellectual curiosity about people and places, was toward engagement rather than condescension. He was interested in Yugoslavia — in its history, its ethnic complexity, its political dynamics — in a way that went beyond professional duty, and the Partisans recognized and responded to that interest.

The sabotage operations that the SOE missions helped plan and coordinate represented one of the most concrete forms of value the British presence provided. Maclean's teams brought with them not just wireless communications and the authority to call in supply drops but technical expertise in demolitions and operational planning that the Partisans could use to maximize the effect of their own considerable energies.

Railway sabotage was the primary focus — the same target set that drove the Jedburgh operations in France and the Wachlarz operations in Poland, for the same fundamental strategic reason: the German military machine ran on rail, and every train that was delayed or derailed was a subtraction from the German capacity to supply, reinforce, and maneuver its forces. In Yugoslavia, the rail network was particularly important because the terrain made road movement slow and costly, meaning that German dependence on the railways was even higher than in more accessible theaters.

The coordination of sabotage operations with Allied air attacks — using the RAF and USAAF aircraft operating from bases in Italy to strike rail infrastructure that the Partisans could not reach or could not destroy with the explosives available on the ground — was one of the most complex coordination challenges the mission faced, and one in which Maclean's direct access to Allied high command proved its value. A wireless message from a Partisan commander identifying a rail junction as a high-value target could, through the mission's communication chain, result in an air strike within days. The combination of ground sabotage and air attack was more effective than either alone, and it was the mission's role to make that combination work.

Maclean's report to Churchill, delivered in person in Cairo in November 1943 after he had been temporarily evacuated from Yugoslavia for consultations, was direct and consequential.

His assessment was unambiguous on the military question: the Partisans were the most effective resistance force in Yugoslavia and were tying down more Axis forces than any other resistance movement in Europe. British support should be switched entirely from the Chetniks to the Partisans, because supporting Mihailović was providing no military benefit and was becoming a positive liability — the evidence of Chetnik collaboration with Axis forces made continued British association with the movement politically and morally untenable.

On the political question — what would happen to Yugoslavia after the war if the Partisans won, given that they were a Communist movement led by a man with deep ties to Moscow — Maclean was characteristically direct. He told Churchill that supporting the Partisans would almost certainly mean a Communist Yugoslavia after the war. Churchill's response, by Maclean's own later account, was to point out that he had no intention of living in Yugoslavia after the war and to confirm that the immediate military requirement — keeping Axis forces occupied in the Balkans — took priority over postwar political calculations.

The decision was made. British support shifted to Tito.

The practical consequences of the decision came quickly. Arms deliveries to the Partisans increased dramatically — the supply drops that had been arriving in modest quantities became a flood of weapons, ammunition, and equipment that transformed the Partisan military capacity in the first months of 1944. The British mission expanded. American OSS officers joined the Allied presence alongside their British SOE counterparts. The Soviets, watching the growing Anglo-American investment in Tito's movement with the mixture of approval and suspicion that characterized Soviet policy toward its Allies throughout the war, dispatched their own mission.

Mihailović was not officially abandoned immediately — the British maintained a liaison mission with him through the early months of 1944, an awkward situation that satisfied no one and that was eventually resolved in the summer of 1944 when the mission was withdrawn and Mihailović's government-in-exile was pressed to remove him from his ministerial position. He was captured by Tito's forces after the war, tried for collaboration and war crimes, and executed in July 1946.

The justice or injustice of that verdict — tried by the government of his political enemies, under legal procedures that did not meet any neutral standard of due process — is one of the enduring disputes of Yugoslav wartime history. What is not disputed is that by the end of the war, the movement he had led had played a marginal military role and a damaging political one, and that the decision Maclean recommended and Churchill made in 1943 had accelerated that marginalization.

Fitzroy Maclean spent the rest of the war in Yugoslavia — returning after his Cairo consultations, participating in the operations that surrounded the Drvar assault, eventually accompanying Tito to Vis and remaining with the Allied mission through the liberation of Belgrade. He was present at moments of historical significance with a consistency that would have seemed improbable had it not been documented by multiple sources.

He wrote about all of it in a book published in 1949 — Eastern Approaches — that became one of the most celebrated British travel and military memoirs of the twentieth century. It is still in print. It is still read. It captures, with the particular literary gift that Maclean brought to everything he did, what it was like to be a young British officer in occupied Yugoslavia in 1943 and 1944 — the mountains and the cold and the fighting and the extraordinary quality of the people who had been living in those mountains and that cold and that fighting for years before any British officer arrived to observe them.

What the book captures less fully — because Maclean was honest about the limits of his own perspective and because some of what he could not fully see became clearer only later — is the full complexity of the political consequences of the decision he recommended. The Communist Yugoslavia that emerged from the war was, by the standards of the Soviet bloc, unusually independent — Tito broke with Stalin in 1948 in a confrontation that could easily have ended in his death but that instead produced a Yugoslavia that charted its own course between the two Cold War blocs. This was not what anyone had predicted in 1943, and it complicates the simple narrative of British support for Tito producing a Soviet satellite.

But it was also not a democracy, and the people who paid the price for that — political opponents imprisoned, Chetnik survivors executed, the postwar reprisals that consumed tens of thousands of lives in the months after liberation — were paying a price that the decision of 1943 had contributed to making inevitable.

Maclean's role in Yugoslav history is remembered differently depending on who is doing the remembering.

In the Yugoslavia that Tito built and in the successor states that emerged from its dissolution, he has been remembered primarily as a friend — the man who recognized the Partisans' worth, who brought British support to a movement that deserved it, and whose personal relationship with Tito helped shape an Alliance that contributed to the liberation of the country. His portrait hung in Yugoslav government buildings. He received Yugoslav decorations alongside his British ones. When he died in 1996, at the age of eighty-five, the obituaries in the former Yugoslav states acknowledged what he had meant to the movement he had assessed and found worthy.

Among Serbs who identify with the Chetnik tradition — and there are many, particularly since the collapse of Communist Yugoslavia and the rehabilitation of Mihailović's reputation that has accompanied it — he is remembered as the man whose report sealed Mihailović's fate and delivered Yugoslavia to Communism. This view, however understandable in its emotional logic, simplifies a decision that was more complex in its context than it appears in retrospect, and attributes to Maclean a decisive influence that properly belonged to Churchill.

The fairest assessment is probably also the most obvious one: that Maclean did what he was sent to do — assessed what he found as accurately and honestly as his perspective and the available evidence allowed — and that the consequences of what he found were shaped by forces and decisions that extended far beyond any single report, however consequential.

He was a man of his time, operating in conditions of extreme complexity, doing his best with what he knew. That is what most of the people in this book were. It is, when the conditions are extreme enough and the stakes high enough, more than sufficient for history to remember.

Operation Ratweek

Destroying the German Retreat

By September 1944 the arithmetic of the war had changed in ways that Germany could no longer reverse.

Romania had defected from the Axis on August 23 — not merely surrendering but switching sides, declaring war on Germany and opening its territory to the Soviet forces that were now advancing westward with a momentum that nothing the Wehrmacht could deploy was going to stop. Bulgaria followed within days. The Soviet armies that had been pressing against the eastern edge of the German position in the Balkans were now moving through territory that had been Axis-controlled weeks earlier, their advance threatening to cut off the entire German force structure in Greece, Albania, and southern Yugoslavia from any connection to the Reich.

Army Group E — the German force responsible for Greece and the southern Balkans, approximately 300,000 men and the equipment of a substantial military formation — faced a withdrawal of nearly a thousand kilometers through terrain that was mountainous, roadbound, and controlled along much of its length by Partisan forces that had been building strength for three years. The withdrawal was not optional. If Army Group E did not move north quickly enough, it would be cut off by the Soviet advance and destroyed in place.

The road north ran through Yugoslavia. Through Tito's Yugoslavia.

The planning for what would become Operation Ratweek began in the Allied headquarters in Italy before the German retreat was fully underway — a product of the intelligence picture that indicated Romania's defection was coming and that the German position in the southern Balkans would become untenable when it did. The operational concept was straightforward in its logic and extraordinarily demanding in its execution: when the Germans began to move north, hit everything they needed to move on, simultaneously and continuously, until the retreat became a catastrophe.

The planning was conducted jointly by the Allied Forces Headquarters in Italy — where Maclean and the British mission maintained their primary connection to the Allied command structure — and by Tito's Partisan high command, which had been developing its own plans for exactly this contingency since the Allied position in Italy had made regular coordination possible. The result was an operation that combined Partisan ground forces, Allied air power, and the SOE mission teams embedded with Partisan units into a coordinated campaign that would have been impossible without the relationships built over the preceding year.

The name Ratweek reflected the contemptuous clarity with which the planners viewed what the operation was designed to achieve: the systematic destruction of an army of rats trying to escape a sinking ship, by blocking every hole through which they might squeeze.

The week designated for the operation's peak intensity was September 1 through 7, 1944 — chosen to coincide with the period when German withdrawal movements were expected to be at their most concentrated. In practice the operation extended well beyond those seven days, as the scale of the German movement and the opportunities it presented proved larger than even optimistic Allied planning had anticipated.

The railway network was the first and highest priority target of Ratweek, and it was attacked with a thoroughness that reflected three years of accumulated Partisan expertise in rail sabotage combined with the technical assistance of SOE demolitions specialists who had been working with Partisan units for months.

The primary rail arteries through Yugoslavia ran north-south through a landscape of river valleys flanked by steep mountain ranges — geography that made the railways indispensable to any large-scale movement of troops and equipment, because the roads that paralleled them were inadequate for the volume of traffic that a retreating army group would generate. A German division that could not use the railway to move its heavy equipment northward faced the choice of abandoning that equipment or moving it by road at a fraction of the speed, consuming fuel it could not reliably replace.

Partisan demolitions teams moved against the railway infrastructure across the length of the Partisan-controlled zone simultaneously — cutting track at multiple points on the same line to prevent the Germans from repairing one cut and resuming operations while the teams were still in the area, destroying locomotive turntables and maintenance facilities that could not be quickly replaced, and targeting the bridges and tunnels on which the lines depended for their routing through the mountain terrain.

The bridge demolitions were the most technically demanding component of the rail sabotage campaign and the most strategically valuable. A cut rail line could be repaired in hours by a competent engineering unit with the right materials. A demolished bridge required days or weeks of repair work, specialized construction equipment, and engineering expertise that the retreating German forces were not configured to provide at scale while simultaneously managing the tactical pressures of a contested withdrawal.

The SOE demolitions specialists worked alongside Partisan engineers to ensure that the bridge attacks were executed with the efficiency that the limited explosive supply required. Placing charges to achieve maximum structural damage with minimum explosive expenditure was a technical skill that training and experience developed and that the Partisan forces had been acquiring steadily since the beginning of British supply. By September 1944 the combination of SOE expertise and Partisan experience had produced demolitions teams capable of dropping a railway bridge with precision — choosing their attack points, placing their charges, and withdrawing before the German security response arrived.

The results of the rail interdiction campaign were visible within days of Ratweek's opening. German formations attempting to use the railway network for their northward movement found line after line closed — not just interrupted but systematically demolished at intervals that made rapid repair impossible. Supply trains that had been scheduled to move medical equipment, ammunition, and fuel northward sat in yards far to the south, unable to reach the units that needed them. The heavy equipment of multiple divisions — artillery, armored vehicles, the mechanical infrastructure of a modern army — began to pile up at rail junctions that could not forward it because the lines ahead were gone.

The road network received simultaneous attention from Partisan ground forces whose three years of experience in ambush and harassment operations gave them capabilities that a conventional army would have taken months of specialized training to develop.

The Yugoslav road network through the mountain corridor of the withdrawal route had characteristics that made it particularly vulnerable to exactly the kind of attack the Partisans excelled at. The roads ran through narrow valleys where the terrain on either side dominated the route — where a small Partisan force occupying the high ground could interdict traffic moving below with firepower disproportionate to the size of the attacking unit. The Germans had to use these roads. They could not effectively suppress the forces firing down on them from positions that were too numerous, too mobile, and too well-concealed to be efficiently attacked by tired units that were trying to move north rather than fight for every kilometer of Yugoslav mountain road.

The ambush operations during Ratweek were not the hit-and-run engagements of the earlier resistance years. They were coordinated attacks, planned in conjunction with the Allied mission teams and timed to achieve maximum effect against specific German formations on specific road segments. A German column that was halted by a road demolition — a blown bridge, a culvert destroyed, a section of road collapsed by explosives — became a stationary target for Partisan forces positioned on the surrounding high ground, who engaged it until it began to move again or until the tactical situation required withdrawal.

The vehicles, equipment, and personnel losses inflicted in these engagements accumulated with a consistency that the German withdrawal command found difficult to manage. Every vehicle destroyed on a mountain road became an obstruction that blocked the vehicles behind it. Every obstruction required engineer effort to clear. Engineer effort devoted to clearing road obstructions was engineer effort not available for bridge repair or defensive construction. The Ratweek campaign was designed to create exactly this kind of cascading demand on German resources — more problems than the retreating force had the capacity to solve simultaneously.

The RAF contribution to Ratweek was conducted primarily by the Balkan Air Force — a combined Allied air command established in June 1944 specifically to support Partisan operations and to exploit the emerging opportunities in the southern Balkans. The Balkan Air Force operated from bases in Italy and drew on aircraft from the RAF, USAAF, South African Air Force, and the Yugoslav Royal Air Force in exile — a genuinely multinational force whose diversity reflected the political complexity of the theater it was supporting.

The air operations during Ratweek complemented the ground sabotage campaign with a precision made possible by the intelligence flowing from the SOE mission teams embedded with Partisan units. A Partisan commander with a British liaison officer could identify a German column halted by a road demolition, relay its location through the mission's wireless, and receive air support within hours — strike aircraft arriving to engage the stationary target before it had been able to clear the obstruction and resume movement.

The targets that the air component struck were selected to maximize the complementarity with the ground operations. Railway yards and marshaling facilities — where the backed-up trains that could not move through demolished lines were accumulating — were attacked from the air with a weight of bombs that the Partisan demolitions teams could not replicate with their available explosives. Fuel storage facilities — already under ground attack where Partisan forces could reach them — received air strikes that destroyed stocks the ground teams had not been able to access. German vehicle columns moving on roads that were under air observation were struck repeatedly, the combination of ground harassment and air attack making movement through certain sections of the withdrawal route so costly that German commanders faced genuine choices about whether to attempt it at all.

The coordination between the air component and the ground operations was imperfect in the ways that all coordination between air and ground forces is imperfect — communication delays, target identification errors, the fog of a rapidly moving tactical situation that made some planned strikes irrelevant by the time the aircraft arrived. But the overall direction of the effect was clear and consistent: every kilometer of the withdrawal route was, during Ratweek, under some form of Allied interdiction, from the air or from the ground or from both simultaneously.

The German withdrawal commanders were experienced professional soldiers who understood their situation with clarity and responded to it with the disciplined professionalism that the Wehrmacht maintained even in its most adverse circumstances. They were not paralyzed by the Ratweek campaign. They continued to move, continued to fight, continued to manage the competing demands of a withdrawal under pressure with the organizational competence that distinguished the German army even in defeat.

But they were slowed. Significantly, measurably, consequentially slowed.

The timeline of Army Group E's withdrawal from Greece to the Yugoslav-Hungarian border — a movement that German planning had estimated could be completed in a matter of weeks under normal conditions — stretched across months of attritional movement that consumed resources and time the German high command could not afford to give it. Formations that were supposed to be available to reinforce the crumbling German front in Hungary by October 1944 were still fighting their way north through Yugoslav mountain passes in November and December, their heavy equipment abandoned or destroyed, their strength depleted by the cumulative losses of an operation that had turned a planned withdrawal into an extended campaign.

The equipment losses alone were strategically significant. The retreating German forces abandoned hundreds of vehicles — trucks, artillery pieces, armored vehicles — that could not be moved through demolished road sections or that were destroyed in Partisan ambushes and air strikes. Each piece of abandoned equipment was not merely a loss to Army Group E but a permanent subtraction from Germany's shrinking military capacity at a moment when the eastern front's demands on that capacity were already unsustainable.

For the Partisan forces conducting Ratweek, the operation represented something qualitatively different from the resistance warfare of the previous three years. They were no longer a clandestine force attacking in secret and then melting back into the landscape. They were a military force in the conventional sense — attacking a retreating enemy army, holding ground, pursuing, blocking — operating with the support of Allied air power and the guidance of Allied mission teams who connected their operations to the broader Allied strategic picture.

The transition was not without its difficulties. Units that had spent years developing the specific skills of guerrilla warfare — patience, concealment, the ability to absorb pressure and survive — had to adapt to the different demands of conventional operations. Commanders who had built their authority in the particular conditions of resistance warfare had to reorient to the different tactical environment of pursuing a retreating army across terrain they controlled.

The Partisan forces managed this transition more successfully than most observers had expected, and the SOE mission teams that had been working with them for the preceding year deserve a share of the credit for that. The professional military exposure that British officers had provided — the tactical planning, the coordination with air support, the systematic thinking about objectives and resources and timelines that conventional military training instills — had given the Partisan commanders tools that resistance warfare alone would not have provided.

Ratweek was the proof of that investment.

The strategic impact of Operation Ratweek cannot be stated in terms of a single decisive battle or a single moment of operational culmination. It was an attritional campaign — its effect measured in the accumulated delay and degradation imposed on a retreating army over weeks and months, rather than in the dramatic rupture of a front or the encirclement of a formation.

Assessed on those terms, its impact was real and significant. Army Group E's withdrawal was delayed by an estimated several months beyond what German planning had anticipated. The formations that eventually reached Hungary arrived depleted in strength, exhausted, and stripped of much of the heavy equipment that had defined their military capacity. They arrived too late to contribute meaningfully to the defense of Hungary in the autumn of 1944, and the state in which they arrived — understrength, under-equipped, physically worn by months of attritional withdrawal — reduced whatever contribution they might have made.

The men who imposed those delays — the Partisan demolitions teams that blew the railway bridges, the ambush groups that halted the road columns, the liaison officers who coordinated the air strikes, the wireless operators who maintained the communication links that made the whole operation function — had done something that three years of resistance warfare had prepared them for without ever quite producing: they had taken a strategic initiative, on a strategic scale, and bent the course of a campaign to their will.

The rats had not escaped cleanly. They had been made to pay for every kilometer of the road north.

In the mathematics of a war that was measured in days and distances and the lives of men, that payment mattered.

The River of No Return

The Battle of the Neretva

In the winter of 1943, Josip Broz Tito made a decision that every military textbook would have told him was insane.

He was trapped. The German high command had assembled for Operation Case White — the fourth major offensive against the Partisans — a force of approximately 90,000 soldiers drawn from German, Italian, and Croatian formations, supported by artillery and air power, designed to encircle and destroy the main Partisan force in a single sustained campaign. The encirclement was closing from the north, the east, and the west. To the south lay the Neretva River — fast, cold, and swollen with winter snowmelt, crossable only at a single bridge that the Partisans still controlled. Behind the bridge, on the far bank, were the Chetniks — Mihailović's forces, theoretically fellow Yugoslav resistance fighters, actually operating in a tactical alliance with the Italian occupation forces that made them, in this situation, enemies.

Tito had 20,000 fighters. He had 4,000 wounded men and women who could not walk unassisted and whom he had publicly and privately committed to not abandoning — a commitment that was not merely sentimental but strategic, because an army that abandoned its wounded was an army that would not recruit, would not inspire loyalty, and would not survive the particular kind of war the Partisans were fighting.

He had one bridge.

His decision: blow it up.

To understand the full weight of what Tito was facing at the Neretva in February 1943, it is necessary to understand what the months preceding the battle had cost the Partisan movement and what its loss would have meant.

The Partisans had spent the preceding year building the organizational and military structures that were transforming them from a guerrilla movement into a conventional military force. The First and Second Offensives had been survived. The liberated territories of Bosnia and Herzegovina had given the movement space to develop — to establish hospitals, schools, administrative structures, the institutional framework of the government-in-arms that Tito was building alongside his army. The Central Hospital — a mobile medical system that moved with the main Partisan force — had thousands of patients, men and women who had been wounded in the operations of the preceding months and who were being treated by Partisan doctors under conditions of considerable difficulty.

The 4,000 wounded in the Central Hospital were not an abstraction. They were people who had been fighting for the Partisan movement, who had been promised that the movement would not leave them behind, and whose fate was known to every fighter in the force. What happened to the wounded if the Partisans were destroyed at the Neretva would not need to be stated — the German and Chetnik treatment of captured Partisans and Partisan wounded was sufficiently well documented that everyone understood exactly what it meant.

Tito's commitment to bring the wounded through was therefore both moral and strategic — a statement about what kind of movement this was, and a guarantee whose maintenance was essential to the trust that kept 20,000 fighters in the field.

Operation Case White — the Germans called it Fall Weiss — had been designed specifically with this encumbrance in mind. The German planners understood that the wounded were the Partisan movement's greatest tactical liability. An army that could move freely could slip through gaps in an encirclement. An army encumbered by 4,000 people who had to be carried could not move freely, and a sufficiently tight encirclement would close before such an army could escape it.

The encirclement that closed around the Partisan main force in the mountains of Herzegovina in January and February 1943 was the tightest the Germans had yet managed. The northern, eastern, and western approaches were blocked by forces strong enough to defeat any frontal attack the Partisans could mount. The Neretva to the south was the only remaining option — and crossing it meant fighting through the Chetniks on the far bank.

The Neretva River in February 1943 was not a river that invited crossing.

It ran through a gorge of considerable depth, its banks steep and in many places effectively vertical, its current swift and powerful with the winter flow that had been fed by snowmelt from the surrounding mountains. The water temperature was close to freezing. The bridge at Jablanica — the single crossing point available to the Partisan force — was a structure capable of bearing the weight of the wounded and their improvised transport, but it was also the only thing standing between the Partisan force and the trap closing around it.

Tito studied the situation with the clinical attention of a commander who has learned, through three years of operating in impossible circumstances, to see tactical possibilities where other commanders see only constraints. What he saw at the Neretva was this: the Germans, applying the conventional logic of military planning, would assume that a force with 4,000 wounded and a single bridge would do everything possible to preserve that bridge. German attention and German planning would therefore be focused on preventing the Partisans from using it — on closing the encirclement before the Partisan force could cross.

What if the Germans were wrong about the bridge?

The plan that Tito developed was a deception of extraordinary boldness. The Partisans would destroy the bridge at Jablanica — deliberately, publicly, in a way the German aerial observers could not miss. The destruction of the bridge would signal to the German high command that the Partisans were not attempting to cross the Neretva — that their movement was in some other direction, that the river was not their intended escape route. German attention would shift northward, to the gap between the closing arms of the encirclement, where the Germans would expect the Partisan breakthrough attempt to come.

Meanwhile, Partisan engineers would construct a makeshift replacement crossing from the wreckage of the destroyed bridge — a temporary structure capable of bearing the weight of wounded on stretchers, not heavy equipment, not vehicles, but people — and the Partisan force would cross it before the Germans realized what was happening.

On the far bank, the Chetniks would have to be defeated. That was not a deception problem. That was a fighting problem. Tito would solve it with the fighters he had.

The bridge at Jablanica was blown on February 8, 1943.

The explosion was visible for miles. German aerial reconnaissance confirmed the destruction. The German operational assessment — recorded in the Wehrmacht's command diaries for the period — noted the bridge's destruction and interpreted it as evidence that the Partisans were not attempting a crossing. German planning adjusted accordingly, with the emphasis of the encirclement shifting to close off what the planners believed were the Partisan movement's likely escape directions.

What German aerial reconnaissance did not observe — because it happened at night, under cover, by men working with the ruins of what had just been destroyed — was the beginning of the improvised reconstruction.

Partisan engineers, working in the gorge below the destroyed bridge, used the structural elements of the demolished span — timber, metal, the physical materials of the bridge itself — to construct a crossing that was, by any engineering standard, barely adequate for its purpose. It was not a bridge in any conventional sense. It was a passage — a series of improvised supports and surfaces spanning the gap left by the demolition, capable of bearing the weight of a person on foot or a stretcher carried by four people, inadequate for anything heavier.

It was enough.

The construction took days — days during which the Partisan security forces maintained the fiction of a force not attempting to cross, while the wounded were prepared for movement and the fighting units were positioned for the assault on the Chetnik forces that would have to be broken on the far bank. The secrecy of the construction, maintained against the ever-present risk of German observation, was itself an operational achievement of the first order — requiring the control of information and movement that the Partisan organizational discipline made possible and that a less disciplined force could not have managed.

The assault across the Neretva and the attack on the Chetnik positions on the far bank began on the night of February 16 to 17, 1943.

The crossing itself was conducted in darkness and under fire — Chetnik forces on the far bank had not been deceived about the Partisan intention to cross and were defending the approaches to the improvised passage with the ferocity of men who understood what would happen to them if the Partisans broke through. The Partisan assault units crossed in the dark, using the improvised structure, and established a foothold on the far bank before the Chetnik defense could be reorganized to drive them back.

The fighting on the far bank was some of the most intense of the entire Neretva campaign. The Chetnik forces defending the crossing point were not negligible — they were experienced fighters in prepared positions, with the advantage of ground and the incentive of knowing that a Partisan breakthrough meant the encirclement they had contributed to would be broken. They fought accordingly.

The Partisan assault units fought harder.

The units chosen for the initial crossing and the assault on the Chetnik positions were among the Partisans' most battle-hardened formations — the First Proletarian Brigade and the Second Proletarian Brigade, the movement's elite infantry, forged in the fighting of the previous two years into formations capable of exactly the kind of sustained close assault that breaking through the Chetnik line required. They attacked with the particular ferocity of fighters who understood that the 4,000 wounded men and women waiting on the near bank would die if the assault failed, and who had decided, with the collective deliberateness of people who had been through enough together to make such decisions collectively, that it would not fail.

The Chetnik line broke. The far bank was secured.

The movement of the wounded across the improvised crossing was the most agonizing phase of the entire operation.

Four thousand people, many of them unable to walk, many of them seriously wounded in ways that made movement excruciating, had to be moved across a makeshift crossing over a freezing river gorge, in winter, under the threat of German air attack and with the sounds of fighting still audible on the far bank as Partisan forces expanded the bridgehead. The movement took days. The medical staff of the Central Hospital — doctors, nurses, orderlies who had been caring for the wounded through months of mountain campaigning — organized the crossing with the same methodical care they brought to everything else, understanding that the crossing was itself a medical event of the first order and that the manner in which it was conducted would determine how many of the wounded survived it.

Some did not survive it. The crossing killed patients whose wounds were too severe to withstand the movement, whose bodies had nothing left to give to the additional demand of being carried across a mountain river on an improvised structure in winter. These deaths were recorded by the Partisan medical service with the same precision that characterized their other records — names, unit, cause of death, date. They are part of the Neretva's accounting, and they belong in it.

The majority of the wounded survived the crossing. This was the central fact of the entire operation — the thing that Tito had staked his tactical deception and his assault force's blood to achieve. The commitment had been kept.

The crossing of the Neretva was not the end of the Partisan ordeal. It was the beginning of the next phase — a fighting withdrawal into the mountains of eastern Bosnia that would continue for weeks, as the German and Italian forces reorganized from the shock of the Partisan breakthrough and resumed the pursuit.

The movement through eastern Bosnia in the weeks following the Neretva crossing was conducted in conditions of extreme physical difficulty. The mountain terrain was snow-covered and in many places passable only on foot. The wounded were still being carried. The pursuing German and Italian forces pressed from behind, and new German formations attempted to establish blocking positions ahead. The Partisan force fought its way through each obstacle with the grim persistence of people who had already survived something that should have destroyed them and who had concluded from that survival that they could survive whatever came next.

The Fifth Offensive — Fall Schwarz, conducted immediately after the Fourth — attempted to finish what Case White had failed to accomplish. It drove the Partisan main force into the mountains of Montenegro and inflicted casualties that brought the movement closer to destruction than any previous offensive had managed. The Partisans lost approximately 7,000 fighters killed in the two offensives — a casualty rate that would have broken most military organizations.

It did not break the Partisans.

The strategic significance of what happened at the Neretva in February and March 1943 extended far beyond the tactical achievement of the crossing itself.

The German high command in Yugoslavia had designed Operation Case White with the specific objective of destroying the Partisan main force — not pushing it back, not forcing it to abandon territory, but eliminating it as a military factor. The operation had committed substantial forces, had achieved significant local successes, and had pressed the Partisan movement to what appeared from the outside to be the point of no return.

And the Partisans had returned anyway.

The psychological impact of this on German military thinking about Yugoslavia was significant and lasting. The assessments that appear in German military documents following the Fourth and Fifth Offensives show a command structure that has concluded — reluctantly, against the grain of its conventional military assumptions — that conventional military operations against the Partisans cannot achieve the decisive result that the German strategic position in the Balkans requires. The Partisans could be hurt, could be pushed, could be bled — but they could not be destroyed by the methods available to the German forces in Yugoslavia, because the methods available were insufficient for the task.

This conclusion did not prevent the Germans from continuing to conduct operations against the Partisans. It did not prevent Operation Rösselsprung, or the various other anti-Partisan actions of 1944. What it did was shift the German strategic calculus — from the expectation that the Partisan problem could be militarily solved to the recognition that it had to be managed, and that the resources required to manage it were a permanent drain on the German military position in a theater that could not be afforded.

The Partisans had demonstrated at the Neretva something that military history reserves as its highest judgment for a fighting force: that they could not be broken. Not by encirclement, not by superior numbers, not by the destruction of their escape routes, not by the abandonment of their wounded — a course that every conventional military calculus would have told Tito was the only rational option. The refusal of that option, and the extraordinary tactical ingenuity with which Tito had made the refusal survivable, had produced a demonstration of military resilience that changed the terms on which the Yugoslav resistance would be fought for the rest of the war.

The bridge at Jablanica — or rather, the ruins of it — became one of the most recognized symbols of the Yugoslav resistance. In Tito's Yugoslavia after the war, the Battle of the Neretva was commemorated with the seriousness that a defining national moment deserves. A museum was established near the site. The battle was the subject of films, books, and educational curricula. The destroyed bridge was preserved as a monument.

This commemoration had the inevitable distortions of official memory — the Communist government's version of the Neretva story emphasized some aspects and suppressed others, particularly the Chetnik role in the encirclement and the moral complexity of fighting fellow Yugoslavs alongside the German and Italian forces. The full history, with all its complexity, was not what official commemoration preferred to remember.

But the core of what it commemorated was real. The crossing of the Neretva was a genuine military achievement of the first order — an act of tactical brilliance under conditions of extreme pressure, executed by a force that had no right to succeed and that succeeded anyway.

The 4,000 wounded who crossed on an improvised structure over a freezing river were the measure of what was accomplished. They crossed because Tito decided they would cross, and because 20,000 fighters agreed to make that decision operational, and because the engineers who built the crossing in the dark from the wreckage of a demolished bridge understood what was being asked of them and delivered it.

They were the shadow army at its most essential — people doing impossible things in impossible conditions because the alternative was a betrayal of everything they had committed themselves to.

The river had not been a river of no return.

They had returned. All of them — the walking, the fighting, and the carried. They had come back from the edge of destruction and kept going north, into the mountains, into the next battle, into the rest of the war.

They had proven something that the Germans would spend the rest of the occupation failing to disprove: that this particular army, in this particular landscape, fighting for this particular cause, was not going to stop.

The Price of Shadows

What Was Won, What Was Lost

The war ended in stages, as wars do.

Germany surrendered on May 8, 1945 — VE Day, Victory in Europe, celebrated in the streets of London and Paris and New York with a joy that was genuine and earned and that contained, for those who looked closely enough, something more complicated than pure triumph. The men and women who had fought in the shadows of occupied Europe did not, for the most part, celebrate in those streets. Many of them were dead. Many were in hospitals. Many were in prisons — not German prisons, but the prisons of the governments that had replaced the German occupation in the east, governments that viewed the resistance fighters of the previous five years with suspicion or outright hostility. Many were simply trying to find their way back to lives that no longer existed in the forms they had left them.

The accounting of what the shadow armies achieved — and what their achievement cost — begins with the military balance sheet, because that is the most tractable part of the ledger. Numbers can be established, or at least approximated. Strategic impact can be assessed, however imperfectly. The human cost can be counted, however incompletely. It is only when the counting is done that the full weight of what these people did and what was done to them begins to be visible.

The strategic contribution of the French Resistance to the Allied victory is most clearly demonstrated in the story this book has told in detail: the seventeen-day delay of the 2nd SS Panzer Division Das Reich on its journey from Toulouse to Normandy.

The military historians who have examined this episode most thoroughly — including Max Hastings, Antony Beevor, and others who have worked directly with German divisional records — are careful about the weight they assign it. The Normandy campaign was decided by many factors. Allied air superiority, the success of Operation Fortitude in deceiving the Germans about the landing site, the failures of German command that kept armored reserves from being committed in the critical first hours — all of these were more structurally significant than the delay of a single division.

But the delay mattered. Das Reich arrived at Normandy after the window in which its intervention might have been decisive had closed. The railway sabotage that caused that delay — conducted by men and women who had been preparing for this moment for years, who acted on coded BBC broadcasts in the middle of the night, who blew bridges and cut rail lines knowing that the reprisals would come — was the direct operational expression of everything SOE and the French Resistance had been building since 1940.

Beyond Das Reich, the broader French Resistance contribution to the D-Day operation — the systematic disruption of German communications, the intelligence provided to Allied planners about German dispositions, the coordination of sabotage operations across the entire rail and road network of occupied France — represented a multiplication of Allied combat power that had no direct conventional military equivalent. The Resistance did not win the Battle of Normandy. But it shaped the conditions in which that battle was won, and the Allied commanders who planned Overlord counted on that contribution in ways that they made explicit in their postwar assessments.

The cost of that contribution was written in the civilian dead of Tulle and Oradour-sur-Glane and dozens of other places across occupied France where the German reprisal machine exacted its payment. 642 people in a village church. 99 men hanging from the balconies of a provincial town. The names run to thousands across the full arc of the occupation, and they are the shadow that falls across every assessment of what the Resistance achieved.

The Polish contribution to the Allied victory was, in certain respects, the most strategically significant of the three theaters examined in this book — and the least recognized in the Western historical memory of the war.

The intelligence coups alone would justify that assessment. The reports that Witold Pilecki smuggled from Auschwitz were among the earliest detailed firsthand accounts of the camp's murder operations to reach Allied hands. The Polish intelligence network that mapped Peenemünde and provided the ground-level confirmation that RAF aerial reconnaissance could not, contributing directly to Operation Hydra and its estimated four-to-six-month delay of the V-2 program. The engineering team that analyzed the crashed

V-2 near the Bug River and flew its secrets to Britain in Operation Most III, advancing Allied understanding of the most technically sophisticated weapon the war produced. The courier network — Jan Karski's journey to Roosevelt, the Cichociemni's two-way traffic between occupied Poland and Britain — that sustained the intelligence link between the underground state and the Allied world through five years of occupation.

The Wachlarz's campaign against German supply lines feeding the Eastern Front was real, if difficult to measure with precision. The sabotage of railway infrastructure, fuel depots, and communication lines across a 1,000-kilometer arc imposed a tax on German logistics that consumed time and resources the Wehrmacht could not afford to spare. The Armia Krajowa's four hundred thousand members tied down German security forces across occupied Poland — forces that were therefore not available for other purposes — for the duration of the occupation.

And then the Warsaw Uprising — the great rising of August 1944 that is beyond this book's specific scope but that cannot be absent from any honest accounting of what the Polish underground cost and achieved. Sixty-three days of street fighting by fighters who had been preparing for exactly this moment. Two hundred thousand dead — fighters and civilians together, in a city that the Germans then systematically destroyed, block by block, as a final act of annihilation. The Soviet forces that could have relieved the uprising waited on the eastern bank of the Vistula while it was crushed.

The underground state that had sustained Polish national identity through five years of deliberate extermination survived the uprising's defeat. Poland survived. Whether that survival justified the cost is a question that Polish historians and Polish families have been answering differently for eighty years, and will continue to answer differently for as long as the question can be asked.

The Yugoslav accounting is perhaps the most complex of the three, because the Yugoslav resistance was simultaneously the most militarily effective resistance movement in occupied Europe and the one whose postwar consequences were most morally ambiguous.

The numbers are not in dispute. At its peak, Tito's Partisan movement numbered 800,000 fighters and tied down more than thirty Axis divisions — German, Italian, Croatian, and Bulgarian forces that were therefore not available for deployment elsewhere. The operations examined in this book — the sabotage campaign against German supply lines, the Battle of the Neretva, Operation Ratweek — were genuine military achievements of strategic significance. The Partisan movement's contribution to the Allied war effort in the Balkans was recognized explicitly by the Allied commanders who supplied and advised it, and it earned that recognition.

The cost was staggering. Approximately one million Yugoslav citizens died during the war — a figure that encompasses Partisan fighters, civilians killed in German reprisals, victims of the Ustaše's ethnic killing program, and casualties of the civil war between Partisans and Chetniks. Yugoslavia lost approximately eleven percent of its prewar population — a proportion exceeded in Europe only by Poland and the Soviet Union. The hundred-civilians-for-every-German-soldier reprisal ratio, applied consistently throughout the occupation, guaranteed that every Partisan military action was paid for in civilian blood at a rate that makes the French and Polish reprisal accounting look, by terrible comparison, moderate.

And the fighters who survived the German occupation found themselves living in a state that was, by any honest description, not what they had been told they were fighting for. The Communist Yugoslavia that emerged from the war was less brutal than Stalin's Soviet Union — Tito's 1948 break with Stalin ensured that the worst features of Soviet-style governance were not fully replicated — but it was a one-party state in which political opposition was imprisoned, in which the press was controlled, in which the postwar reprisals against perceived enemies consumed tens of thousands of lives in the months after liberation. The Partisans who had fought against one form of authoritarian occupation found themselves living under a different one, administered by the movement they had built.

This is not a verdict on whether fighting was the right choice. Given what the occupation was doing to Yugoslavia — the Ustaše's killing program, the German reprisal massacres, the deliberate destruction of civilian infrastructure — the alternative to fighting was not peace. It was a different and probably worse form of destruction. But it is a recognition that the world the Yugoslav fighters built with their blood was not the world they had imagined when they answered Tito's call in the summer of 1941.

The individual postwar fates of the resistance fighters this book has followed deserve to be stated plainly, because they are the most honest measure of what the shadow armies ultimately received in return for what they gave.

Vera Atkins — who had briefed SOE's agents in the small hours before their flights into occupied France, who had tracked their fates with obsessive devotion, who had spent years after the war attending war crimes trials and piecing together the final hours of the people she had dispatched into the darkness — returned to a Britain that had no official mechanism for acknowledging what she had done. Her role in F Section was classified. Her contribution was not publicly recognized for decades. She worked in obscurity in the post-war years, the knowledge of what she knew and what she had carried locked inside her, until the gradual declassification of SOE records began to allow the history to be written.

Nancy Wake received her decorations — the George Medal, the Médaille de la Résistance, the American Medal of Freedom — and found that they were not sufficient substitute for the life the war had taken from her. Henri Fiocca was dead. The Marseille world she had inhabited was gone. She spent decades in a kind of restless displacement that the decorations did not resolve and the memoirs did not fully capture. She died in London in 2011, ninety-eight years old, the last survivor of a world that had ceased to exist before most of the people who read about it were born.

Francis Suttill died at Sachsenhausen in March 1945, thirty days before it was liberated. Andrée Borrel died at Natzweiler in July 1944, twenty-nine years old, injected with phenol and cremated while still alive. Jean Moulin died in German custody in July 1943, under torture that the postwar record has never been able to fully describe because none of the people who inflicted it were made to describe it in sufficient detail. The agents of the Prosper network who were captured and transported to concentration camps died in ones and twos across the German camp system in the final years of the war, their names recovered by Vera Atkins' postwar investigations and placed in the record that their stories deserved.

The Polish accounting after the war was, if possible, even more painful than during it.

Witold Pilecki — who had voluntarily entered Auschwitz, organized resistance from within the camp, smuggled intelligence to the outside world, escaped after 947 days, participated in the Warsaw Uprising, survived German captivity, and returned to Poland after liberation — was arrested by the Communist secret police in 1947, tortured, tried on fabricated charges, and executed with a single bullet to the back of the head in May 1948. He was forty-seven years old.

He was not alone. The AK fighters who had survived five years of German occupation found themselves hunted by the UB — the Communist security service — in the years after liberation. Former AK members were arrested, imprisoned, and in some cases executed under charges of anti-state activity that would have seemed obscene to anyone who understood what anti-state activity had looked like in Poland between 1939 and 1944. The underground state that had sustained Polish national identity through the occupation was dissolved. Its leaders were imprisoned or driven into exile. The history of what they had built was suppressed and distorted for decades by a government that preferred a different account of the war.

The Cichociemni who survived the German occupation were not safe in the Poland that followed it. Elżbieta Zawacka — the only woman among the 316, the courier and parachutist whose wartime service had taken her across occupied Europe and back — was arrested by the UB in 1951 and held for three years. She survived. Many of her comrades did not.

Jan Karski — who had risked everything to bring the truth about Auschwitz to Roosevelt and Churchill, who had done everything that a single human being could do to make the Allied governments understand and act on what was happening in occupied Poland — spent the postwar decades in academic life in the United States, carrying the knowledge of what he had seen and what the world had done with his testimony. He did not return to live in Poland. The Poland he had served no longer existed in the form he had served.

The shadow armies achieved what they set out to achieve. That statement can be made with the confidence that the historical record, imperfect as it is, provides.

France was liberated. The German occupation that had seemed, in the summer of 1940, like a permanent feature of European life was gone in four years, expelled by Allied armies that the Resistance had helped to make effective. The men and women who blew the railway bridges and kept the Maquis supplied and walked through German checkpoints with forged documents in their pockets contributed to that liberation in ways that are documented and real. They did not win the war. They helped win it, at a cost that the history books have never fully discharged.

Poland survived. The underground state that the Germans had designed to be destroyed — the schools, the courts, the press, the cultural institutions, the four hundred thousand fighters of the Armia Krajowa — had kept Polish national identity alive through five years of deliberate extermination. When the occupation ended, Poland was still there — still Polish, still capable of reconstituting itself as a nation, still in possession of the cultural and intellectual inheritance that the AB-Aktion had tried to destroy at the beginning of the occupation. The Communist government that followed the German occupation suppressed and distorted this history for decades. The history survived the suppression, as Polish things had a way of surviving what was done to them.

Yugoslavia was liberated. The Partisan movement that began with a few hundred fighters in the summer of 1941 and grew to 800,000 by 1944 had expelled the German occupation and built, in its place, a state that was — whatever its faults and whatever the human cost of its construction — Yugoslav rather than German. The country that emerged from the war was not the country that had existed before April 1941. It was something new, built from the experience of resistance and civil war and the particular political vision of the man who had led both. Its ultimate fate — the dissolution of Yugoslavia in the wars of the 1990s — belongs to a different history. What belongs here is that it existed, that it was free, and that its freedom was purchased in the mountains and the river crossings and the blown railway bridges of the years examined in this book.

What is the right way to end a book about people who fought in the dark?

Not with triumph. The facts do not support a triumphalist conclusion, and the people who lived these facts deserved better than to have their stories reduced to a clean narrative of sacrifice rewarded. Witold Pilecki was not rewarded. The Prosper agents who died in concentration camps were not rewarded. The 642 civilians of Oradour-sur-Glane were not rewarded. The million Yugoslav dead were not rewarded in any sense that the word can bear.

Not with despair, either. The facts do not support that conclusion either, and the people who lived them did not despair — or if they did, they despaired and kept fighting, which is a different thing entirely and a more important one.

What the facts support is something more honest and more difficult than either triumph or despair: the recognition that these people did something that mattered, at a cost that was real and permanent, in conditions that most human beings will never face and that no human being should be asked to face, and that the world they helped to preserve is the world we continue to live in.

They were not heroes in the simplified sense that the word is usually deployed — the sense that implies clarity of purpose, certainty of outcome, and a clean relationship between sacrifice and reward. They were people — farmers and teachers and lawyers and students and cavalry officers and journalists and librarians — who were placed by the accident of history in circumstances that demanded more of them than circumstances have any right to demand, and who met that demand as completely as human beings are capable of meeting it.

Some of them survived. Many did not. Those who survived often found that what they had survived for was not what they had imagined when they made their choice to fight. The postwar world was not the world they had been promised. History never delivers the world that the people who make it are promised.

What it delivered, in this case, was enough. Not what they deserved. Not what they had earned. But enough.

There is a specific quality to the courage of people who fight in the dark — who operate without the visible structure of an army, without the support of comrades in arms who can see what you are doing and validate your sacrifice, without the institutional framework that gives conventional soldiers their identity and their purpose.

The conventional soldier fights within a system that acknowledges his fighting. His uniform announces his role. His rank places him in a hierarchy. His unit provides him with community. If he dies, there are procedures — notification of next of kin, the recording of his death in official records, the preservation of his identity in the institutional memory of the service that claimed him.

The resistance fighter has none of this. She operates under a false name. Her role is acknowledged by no one except the small number of people who know what she is doing. If she is captured, the organization she belongs to will deny her — not out of betrayal but out of operational necessity, the same compartmentalization that gives the network its resilience. If she dies, the record of her death may never be found. Her real name may not appear in any document accessible to the people who loved her.

Vera Atkins spent years after the war finding these people — tracking down the fates of the agents she had sent into France, attending trials, reading German records, piecing together final hours from the testimony of survivors and perpetrators alike. She did it because someone had to, and because the alternative — allowing these people to simply disappear into the historical silence of the unrecorded — was intolerable to her.

The book you have just read is, in a smaller and more distant way, an extension of the same project. Not a recovery of what was lost — too much is irretrievably lost for that — but an insistence that what can be recovered should be, and that the people who did these things in the dark deserve to be seen, as clearly and as honestly as the historical record allows, in the light.

The dedication of this book names them: the shadow fighters of France, Poland, and Yugoslavia — the farmers and teachers, the students and librarians, the ordinary people who chose an extraordinary path when darkness fell across their world.

They carried no flags and wore no uniforms. They fought alone, in secret, and often died the same way.

History remembers the generals.

This book is for the rest.

Glossary

The Shadow Wars Series

The following glossary covers the key organizations, agencies, terms, and operational concepts that appear across the Shadow Wars Series. Entries are arranged alphabetically. Readers encountering an unfamiliar term while reading any volume in the series will find a plain-language explanation here.

A

A Force — British military deception unit based in Cairo during World War II, responsible for strategic deception operations in the Middle East and North Africa, including Operation Bertram, which contributed to the success of the Second Battle of El Alamein in 1942.

Abwehr — Germany's military intelligence service, operating from 1920 to 1944 under the German Armed Forces High Command. Responsible for espionage, counterintelligence, and sabotage operations. Disbanded by Hitler in 1944 and its functions absorbed by the SS and SD after Admiral Wilhelm Canaris, its longtime chief, fell under suspicion.

Agent — In intelligence terminology, a person who gathers information or performs operations on behalf of an intelligence service. Distinct from an "officer," who is a professional employee of the intelligence organization. An agent may be a foreign national, a recruited civilian, or anyone working under the direction of an intelligence service.

AK (Armia Krajowa) — The Home Army. The dominant Polish resistance movement during World War II, operating under the command of the Polish government-in-exile in London. At its peak one of the largest underground resistance organizations in occupied Europe, conducting sabotage, intelligence gathering, and armed operations against the German occupation.

Alliance Network — The largest French intelligence network of World War II, run by Marie-Madeleine Fourcade and known internally as Noah's Ark. Operated throughout the German occupation of France, providing extensive intelligence about German naval and military operations to British intelligence.

Armistice — A formal agreement to stop fighting, typically as a prelude to a peace treaty. In the context of this series, refers primarily to the armistice of November 11, 1918, ending World War I, and the armistice of June 22, 1940, between Germany and France following the German invasion, which established the Vichy French government.

Asset — An intelligence term for a person, organization, or resource that provides useful information or services to an intelligence operation. A human asset is a person providing intelligence or assistance, whether voluntarily, for payment, or under coercion.

Ausweis — A German identity document or pass, required under German occupation in much of Europe during World War II. Different types of Ausweis granted different levels of movement and access. The ability to produce a convincing forged Ausweis was critical to the survival of agents and Jews fleeing persecution in occupied Europe.

B

BCRA (Bureau Central de Renseignements et d'Action) — The Central Bureau of Intelligence and Operations. The Free French intelligence and special operations service, established in London in 1942 under the direction of General de Gaulle's government in exile. Coordinated French resistance intelligence activities and liaison with British SOE and American OSS.

Black propaganda — Disinformation or propaganda that conceals or misrepresents its true origin, typically making it appear to come from a source it does not. Used extensively by both Allied and Axis powers during World War II to undermine enemy morale, spread confusion, or manipulate enemy decision-making.

Blown — Intelligence slang for an agent or operation whose cover has been compromised and is known to the opposing intelligence service. A blown agent is in immediate danger and must be extracted or go into hiding. A blown operation must be abandoned.

Burned — Intelligence slang for an agent who has been identified by hostile counterintelligence and can no longer operate safely in a given environment. A burned agent may be deliberately exposed by their own service when they are no longer useful, or may be identified through their own mistakes or through enemy penetration of their network.

C

CIA (Central Intelligence Agency) — The United States' principal foreign intelligence service, established in 1947 as the successor to the wartime Office of Strategic Services (OSS). Responsible for collecting, analyzing, and disseminating foreign intelligence and conducting covert operations abroad. Headquartered in Langley, Virginia.

Cipher — A system for encrypting information by substituting or transposing letters or symbols according to a predetermined key. Distinguished from a code, in which entire words or phrases are replaced by other words or symbols. Ciphers were the primary method of securing military and intelligence communications throughout both World Wars and the Cold War.

Clandestine operation — An operation conducted in secret, with its existence concealed from those not involved. In intelligence terminology, distinguished from a covert operation, in which the operation may be acknowledged but the sponsoring organization is concealed.

Cold War — The period of geopolitical tension between the United States and its Western allies and the Soviet Union and its Eastern bloc partners, lasting from approximately 1947 to the dissolution of the Soviet Union in 1991. Characterized by ideological conflict, proxy wars, nuclear arms race, and extensive espionage by both sides, but no direct military conflict between the superpowers.

Compartmentalization — A security practice in which information is divided into separate compartments, with each person or unit knowing only what is necessary for their specific function. Standard practice in intelligence operations to limit the damage caused by the capture or betrayal of any individual agent.

Composition C (C-4) — A plastic explosive compound developed in Britain during World War II and used extensively by SOE agents and resistance networks for sabotage operations. The predecessor of modern C-4 explosive. Its plasticity allowed it to be shaped to fit specific targets, making it far more versatile than earlier explosive compounds.

Counterintelligence — Intelligence activities designed to identify, neutralize, and exploit the intelligence operations of foreign powers or hostile organizations. Includes surveillance of suspected agents, penetration of enemy intelligence services, and the running of double agents.

Courier — A person who physically transports intelligence materials, documents, or other sensitive items between agents or between agents and their handlers. Courier work is among the most dangerous functions in a clandestine network, as capture means arrest with incriminating materials in hand.

Cover — A false identity or explanation adopted by an agent to conceal their true purpose or affiliation. A cover story is the explanation an agent provides for their presence, activities, or identity. Cover may be shallow (a simple false name) or deep (a fully constructed false biography supported by forged documents and a verifiable history).

Covert operation — An operation in which the sponsoring organization's involvement is concealed, even if the operation itself may eventually become known. Distinct from a clandestine operation, in which both the operation and its sponsorship are secret.

Croix de Guerre — A French military decoration established during World War I and awarded for acts of valor in the presence of enemy forces. One of the highest French military honors, awarded to numerous resistance fighters, SOE agents, and intelligence operatives including Virginia Hall and Josephine Baker.

D

D-Day — Military terminology for the day on which a combat operation begins. In common usage, refers specifically to June 6, 1944, the date of the Allied amphibious landings in Normandy, France — the largest seaborne invasion in history, which opened the Western Front against Germany.

Dead drop — A method of passing intelligence materials between agents without direct personal contact. Materials are left at a prearranged location (the "drop") by one party and collected by another, reducing the risk that both parties will be observed together. Widely used during the Cold War.

Defector — A person who abandons their country, cause, or allegiance, typically to join or provide information to an opposing power. Intelligence defectors are particularly valuable because they bring firsthand knowledge of the organizations they have left.

Deuxième Bureau — The Second Bureau. France's military intelligence service, operating throughout World War I and into World War II. Responsible for foreign intelligence collection and analysis. Effectively dissolved after the fall of France in 1940, with its functions split between Vichy French intelligence and the Free French BCRA.

Direction finding (DF) — A technique for locating a radio transmitter by triangulating its signal using multiple receiving stations or mobile units. German direction-finding vans were a primary threat to clandestine radio operators in occupied Europe during World War II. A transmitting agent typically had twenty minutes to two hours before direction-finding equipment could pinpoint their location.

Double agent — An agent who ostensibly works for one intelligence service while secretly working for another. Double agents may be genuine defectors who maintain contact with their original service, agents who have been turned after capture, or agents deliberately planted to deceive the opposing service. Among the most valuable and dangerous figures in intelligence operations.

DS (Durzhavna Sigurnost) — The Bulgarian State Security service, the communist-era intelligence and secret police organization of Bulgaria. Closely aligned with the KGB and responsible for several Cold War-era operations in Western Europe, including the 1978 assassination of Bulgarian dissident Georgi Markov in London.

E

Electric Fence (High Voltage Fence) — The electrified wire barrier erected by the German occupation authorities along the Belgian-Dutch and Franco-Belgian borders during World War I and again during World War II. Designed to prevent the unauthorized movement of people and information across the frontier. The fence was lethal and claimed the lives of numerous agents and civilians attempting to cross.

Englandspiel — The England Game. A German Abwehr deception operation conducted in the Netherlands from 1942 to 1944, in which captured SOE agents were forced to transmit back to London under German control. The operation resulted in fifty-four Allied agents being sent into German-controlled territory and captured on arrival. One of the most successful counterintelligence operations of World War II.

Exfiltration — The clandestine removal of an agent or other person from a hostile or denied area. The covert equivalent of evacuation. Exfiltration routes during World War II typically ran through neutral countries such as Spain, Sweden, or Switzerland.

F

F Section — The French Section of the British Special Operations Executive, responsible for operations in France independent of the Free French government-in-exile. Distinct from the RF Section, which coordinated with the Free French. F Section deployed over 400 agents into France during World War II, including many of the women whose stories appear in this series.

FBI (Federal Bureau of Investigation) — The United States' domestic intelligence and law enforcement agency, responsible for counterintelligence within US borders. During World War II, the FBI under J. Edgar Hoover was responsible for identifying enemy agents operating in the United States, including the investigation of Velvalee Dickinson's doll code operation.

Free French — The French government-in-exile and its associated military forces, established by General Charles de Gaulle in London following the fall of France in June 1940. Continued the fight against Germany from abroad and coordinated with the French resistance inside occupied France through the BCRA.

Fuze (or Fuse) — A device used to detonate an explosive charge after a set period of time or upon specific stimulus. In SOE and OSS sabotage operations, time-delay fuzes allowed agents to set charges and leave the area before detonation. The reliability of the fuze was critical — an early detonation killed the agent, a late one gave the enemy time to find and disarm the charge.

G

George Cross (GC) — The second-highest British civilian decoration, awarded for acts of the greatest heroism or most conspicuous courage in circumstances of extreme danger. Awarded posthumously to Noor Inayat Khan and Violette Szabo, among other SOE agents.

Gestapo (Geheime Staatspolizei) — The Secret State Police of Nazi Germany, established in 1933. Responsible for investigating and suppressing resistance and opposition to the Nazi regime. In occupied Europe, the Gestapo was the primary threat to resistance networks and Allied agents, known for brutal interrogation methods and the systematic arrest and execution of captured operatives.

GRU (Glavnoye Razvedyvatelnoye Upravleniye) — The Main Intelligence Directorate of the Soviet Armed Forces. The Soviet military intelligence service, distinct from the civilian KGB and its predecessors. Throughout the Cold War, the GRU ran extensive networks of agents in Western countries focused on military and technical intelligence. Officers of the GRU include Ruth Werner (codename Sonya) and the members of the Richard Sorge spy ring.

H

Handler — An intelligence officer responsible for managing and directing an agent or network of agents. The handler provides instructions, receives intelligence, arranges communication, and is responsible for the agent's security and welfare. The handler-agent relationship is the fundamental operational unit of human intelligence collection.

Honey trap (also: honey pot) — An intelligence operation in which a romantic or sexual relationship is used to compromise, recruit, or extract information from a target. Used by multiple intelligence services throughout the period covered by this series. The KGB's systematic use of female officers in this role gave rise to the term "Swallow" for female operatives and "Raven" for male ones.

I

Illegal — In Soviet intelligence terminology, an officer or agent operating in a foreign country without diplomatic cover, using a false identity and without the protection of diplomatic immunity. Distinct from a "legal," who operates under diplomatic cover. Illegals are more difficult to identify but face severe consequences if captured, as they have no official status to protect them.

Infiltration — The covert insertion of an agent or agents into enemy-held territory or into a target organization. During World War II, SOE and OSS agents were typically infiltrated into occupied Europe by parachute, by small boat, or by crossing land borders using false identity documents.

Intelligence — Information that has been collected, analyzed, and evaluated for use by decision-makers. In military and governmental contexts, intelligence refers both to the information itself and to the organizations and processes that produce it. Raw information becomes intelligence through the process of analysis and assessment.

Invisible ink — A substance used to write messages that are invisible under normal conditions but can be revealed through application of heat, light, or a chemical developer. Used throughout the period covered by this series to conceal intelligence messages in apparently innocent correspondence. Josephine Baker used invisible ink to write intelligence on her sheet music.

Iron Curtain — The political, military, and ideological boundary dividing Europe between the Western democratic nations and the Soviet-dominated Eastern bloc during the Cold War. The term was popularized by Winston Churchill in a 1946 speech. Along the Iron Curtain's physical manifestations — the Berlin Wall, the fortified borders between East and West — much of the Cold War's human drama played out.

J

Jedburgh teams — Three-person teams of Allied officers (typically one American, one British, and one French) parachuted into occupied France ahead of the D-Day landings to organize, train, and coordinate resistance operations.

Named after the Scottish town where they trained. Operated in coordination with both SOE and OSS.

K

Kamera — Also known as Special Bureau Number One. The KGB laboratory responsible for developing poisons and other assassination compounds for use in Soviet intelligence operations. Established under Stalin and continued in various forms through the Soviet period. Responsible for the ricin pellet used to assassinate Bulgarian dissident Georgi Markov in London in 1978.

KGB (Komitet Gosudarstvennoy Bezopasnosti) — The Committee for State Security. The Soviet Union's principal security and intelligence agency from 1954 to 1991, responsible for both foreign intelligence collection and domestic security. The KGB was the successor to a series of earlier Soviet security organizations including the NKVD, NKGB, and MGB. Dissolved following the collapse of the Soviet Union in 1991, its functions divided among successor organizations including the FSB and SVR.

Kennkarte — The German identity card issued to inhabitants of occupied territories during World War II, containing the bearer's name, date and place of birth, physical description, photograph, thumbprint, and signature. One of the primary documents that Allied forgers worked to replicate. A convincing forged Kennkarte was essential to any agent operating under cover in German-occupied Europe.

L

La Dame Blanche — The White Lady. A Belgian and French intelligence network of approximately 1,000 agents that operated during World War I, providing British military intelligence with extensive information about German troop and railway movements through systematic observation. One of the most productive Allied intelligence networks of the war, with women constituting a significant portion of its membership.

Légion d'honneur — The Legion of Honor. France's highest order of merit, established by Napoleon Bonaparte in 1802. Awarded to military personnel and civilians for exceptional service to France. Received by several subjects of this series including Virginia Hall, Josephine Baker, and Marie-Madeleine Fourcade.

Limpet mine — A type of naval mine attached to a ship's hull by magnets, detonated by a time-delay fuze. Developed by SOE's Station IX and used extensively by Allied frogmen and resistance operatives to sink or damage enemy shipping without direct combat. The name derives from the limpet shellfish, which attaches firmly to rocks.

M

Manhattan Project — The American-led research and development program, conducted during World War II with British and Canadian participation, that produced the world's first nuclear weapons. Operated from 1942 to 1946 under conditions of extreme secrecy. Soviet intelligence penetration of the Manhattan Project — primarily through the networks of Klaus Fuchs, Julius Rosenberg, and others — provided the Soviet Union with significant technical information that accelerated its own nuclear weapons program.

MBE (Member of the Order of the British Empire) — A British honor awarded for significant achievement or service to the community. Among the lower tier of the Order of the British Empire. Awarded to Christine Granville (Krystyna Skarbek) for her wartime service, alongside the George Cross and the Croix de Guerre.

MI5 (Military Intelligence, Section 5) — The United Kingdom's domestic counterintelligence and security agency, formally known as the Security Service. Responsible for identifying and neutralizing threats to British national security from within the United Kingdom, including foreign intelligence operations on British soil. During World War II, MI5 ran the Double Cross System, turning captured German agents into double agents.

MI6 (Military Intelligence, Section 6) — The United Kingdom's foreign intelligence service, formally known as the Secret Intelligence Service (SIS). Responsible for collecting intelligence outside the United Kingdom. Distinct from MI5, which handles domestic security. The organization whose wartime penetration by Kim Philby represents one of the Cold War's most damaging intelligence failures.

Microfilm — A photographic technique that reduces documents or images to a tiny fraction of their original size, allowing large amounts of information to be concealed in very small objects. Widely used in Cold War intelligence operations to pass classified documents. The hollow nickel used by Soviet spy Rudolf Abel contained a microfilm image.

Mitrokhin Archive — A collection of handwritten notes and transcriptions of KGB files made secretly by KGB archivist Vasili Mitrokhin over a period of years and brought to Britain when he defected in 1992. The archive provided Western intelligence services with an unprecedented view into KGB operations spanning decades. Published in two volumes by Christopher Andrew and Vasili Mitrokhin as The Mitrokhin Archive (1999) and The Mitrokhin Archive II (2005).

Mole — An agent who has penetrated an enemy organization from within, typically by being recruited before joining the target organization or very early in their career. Distinguished from a defector or walk-in by the long-term, premeditated nature of the penetration. The Cambridge Spy

Ring represents the most famous example of mole penetration in British intelligence history.

N

Nacht und Nebel (Night and Fog) — A directive issued by Hitler in December 1941, ordering that certain prisoners — primarily resistance fighters and spies from occupied Western Europe — be made to "disappear" into the German security apparatus without any information being provided to their families or governments. Nacht und Nebel prisoners were typically transported to concentration camps in Germany, kept in isolation, and their fates kept secret. Noor Inayat Khan was classified as a Nacht und Nebel prisoner.

Network — In intelligence terminology, an organized group of agents working together under common direction to collect intelligence or conduct operations. Also called a circuit or cell structure. Most resistance and intelligence networks were compartmentalized so that the arrest of one member could not reveal the entire network.

NKVD (Narodnyy Komissariat Vnutrennikh Del) — The People's Commissariat for Internal Affairs. A Soviet security and intelligence organization that served multiple functions including secret police, intelligence collection, and administration of the Gulag labor camp system. The NKVD's foreign intelligence functions were among its most significant activities during the 1930s and 1940s. Reorganized multiple times and eventually replaced by the KGB in 1954.

O

Office of Strategic Services (OSS) — The United States' wartime intelligence and special operations agency, established in 1942 under the direction of General William "Wild Bill" Donovan. The OSS conducted intelligence collection, analysis, sabotage, and subversion operations in both the European and Pacific theaters. Dissolved at the end of World War II, its functions eventually transferred to the newly created CIA in 1947.

Official Secrets Act — British legislation criminalizing the unauthorized disclosure of information related to national security or intelligence activities. The Official Secrets Act bound all SOE and MI6 personnel and agents, preventing them from publicly discussing their wartime activities for decades after the war. Many participants in the events described in this series carried their knowledge in silence for the rest of their lives as a direct result of this legislation.

One-time pad — An encryption system in which the key used to encrypt a message is as long as the message itself and is used only once. When properly implemented, the one-time pad is mathematically unbreakable. Used by Soviet intelligence for communication with agents in the field. The hollow nickel used by Rudolf Abel contained a one-time pad key in microfilm form.

Operation Bernhard — The Nazi program to destabilize the British economy by flooding it with forged Bank of England notes, executed using Jewish prisoners at Sachsenhausen concentration camp from 1942 to 1945. Produced between £130 million and £150 million in forged notes. Named after its supervisor, SS officer Bernhard Krüger.

Operation Mincemeat — A British deception operation conducted in 1943, in which the corpse of a homeless Welsh man was dressed as a British Royal Marines officer and floated off the coast of Spain carrying forged documents suggesting Allied plans to invade Greece and Sardinia rather than Sicily. The deception succeeded in misleading German intelligence about the actual Allied invasion target.

Operation Torch — The Allied invasion of French North Africa in November 1942, the first major Allied offensive in the Western theater. The operation's success was aided by intelligence gathered by OSS agent Amy Thorpe, whose acquisition of Vichy French naval ciphers gave Allied planners critical information about French naval dispositions.

P

Penetration — The successful insertion of an agent into a target organization for the purpose of collecting intelligence or conducting influence operations from within. The penetration of Allied intelligence networks by German counter-intelligence — and the penetration of Western intelligence services by Soviet agents — are central themes throughout this series.

Plastic explosive — An explosive compound with a clay-like consistency that can be shaped by hand to fit specific targets. Its malleability makes it far more versatile than rigid explosive compounds for sabotage applications. Composition C (the British formulation) and its successor C-4 (the American formulation) were the standard plastic explosives used by SOE and OSS operatives.

Propaganda — Information, especially of a biased or misleading nature, used to promote a particular political cause or point of view. Both Allied and Axis powers invested heavily in propaganda operations during World War II, targeting both civilian populations and military personnel. White propaganda acknowledges its source; black propaganda disguises or misrepresents it.

R

Radio game — A deception operation in which a captured agent's radio is operated by the capturing intelligence service to feed false information to the agent's original handlers. The German Englandspiel operation in the Netherlands is the most extensively documented example of this technique during World War II.

Raven — KGB terminology for a male intelligence officer used in seduction operations against female targets. The female equivalent was called a Swallow. Part of the systematic KGB program using personal relationships as an intelligence tool against Western targets.

Resistance — Organized opposition to enemy occupation or control. During World War II, resistance movements operated throughout German-occupied Europe, conducting intelligence collection, sabotage, escape line operations, and eventually armed action against the occupying forces. Resistance networks were supplied and supported by SOE and OSS and were central to Allied intelligence collection efforts.

Ricin — A highly toxic compound derived from castor beans, with no known antidote. Used by the KGB in the 1978 assassination of Bulgarian dissident Georgi Markov in London, delivered via a platinum pellet fired from a modified umbrella. One of the most lethal naturally occurring poisons known.

S

Sabotage — Deliberate destruction of or damage to an enemy's equipment, infrastructure, or resources. A primary function of SOE and OSS operations in occupied Europe during World War II, targeting railways, industrial facilities, communications infrastructure, and military equipment to disrupt German war production and logistics.

SD (Sicherheitsdienst) — The Security Service of the SS, serving as the intelligence agency of the Nazi Party and the SS. Responsible for gathering intelligence about threats to the regime and, in occupied territories, identifying and suppressing resistance activities. The SD worked closely with the Gestapo in occupied Europe.

Security check — A prearranged signal embedded in an agent's radio transmissions to indicate that they are operating freely and not under enemy control. If the security check was absent from a transmission, it was supposed to alert the receiving station that the agent had been captured and was transmitting under duress. Failures to act on absent security checks contributed to several intelligence disasters during World War II.

SOE (Special Operations Executive) — Britain's clandestine sabotage and intelligence organization, established in 1940 on Churchill's instruction to "set Europe ablaze." The SOE trained and inserted agents into occupied Europe and Asia to conduct sabotage, support resistance networks, and gather intelligence. Employed both men and women as agents, and was at the forefront of developing the tools and techniques of covert warfare. Dissolved in 1946.

Sorge Ring — The Soviet spy network operated by Richard Sorge in Shanghai and subsequently in Tokyo from the early 1930s until its discovery in 1941. One of the most productive Soviet intelligence operations of the period, providing Moscow with critical information about Japanese and German military intentions. Agnes Smedley assisted in establishing the network's Shanghai phase.

SS (Schutzstaffel) — The Protection Squadron. Originally Hitler's personal bodyguard unit, the SS grew into a vast military, police, and administrative organization that was central to the operation of the Nazi state and the Holocaust. The SS encompassed the Gestapo, the SD, the concentration camp system, and the Waffen-SS military units, among other functions.

Station IX — The SOE's primary research and development facility, housed at The Frythe, a converted country hotel in Welwyn, Hertfordshire. The site where the suitcase radios, explosive coal, concealment devices, and other tools of the secret war were designed, built, and tested. Operated throughout World War II under conditions of strict secrecy.

Sten gun — A British submachine gun developed in 1941 and manufactured in large quantities for distribution to resistance networks and Allied forces. Deliberately designed for simplicity and cheapness, the Sten could be produced with minimal tooling and could be disassembled into components small enough to be carried covertly. Its reliability was variable, but its availability and concealability made it the primary weapon of the European resistance.

Swallow — KGB terminology for a female intelligence officer used in seduction operations against male targets. The male equivalent was called a Raven. The KGB's Second Chief Directorate maintained a systematic program using both Swallows and Ravens to compromise or recruit Western officials in Moscow and elsewhere during the Cold War.

T

Tradecraft — The techniques and methods used by intelligence officers and agents to conduct their operations while avoiding detection. Includes methods of communication, surveillance detection, cover maintenance, dead drop procedures, and the full range of operational skills required for clandestine work.

Triangulation — The process of determining the location of a radio transmitter by taking directional readings from two or more receiving points and finding their intersection. The basis of the direction-finding operations used by German security services to locate clandestine radio operators in occupied Europe.

Tube Alloys — The British wartime nuclear weapons research program, the predecessor of the joint British-American effort that became the Manhattan Project. Tube Alloys research produced technical information that was passed to Soviet intelligence by agents including Melita Norwood and Klaus Fuchs.

Turned agent — An agent who has been captured by an opposing intelligence service and persuaded or coerced to work for that service, typically by continuing to operate against their original employers under the direction of the capturing service. Mathilde Carré (La Chatte) is among the most documented examples of a turned agent in the World War II period.

U

U-boat (Unterseeboot) — German submarine. U-boats conducted an extended campaign against Allied shipping in the Atlantic throughout World War II, threatening to cut Britain's supply lines. Intelligence about U-boat operations, gathered in part through agents like Marthe Richer, was critical to Allied efforts to counter the submarine campaign.

V

Venona — A long-running US signals intelligence program that intercepted and decrypted Soviet intelligence communications between 1943 and 1980. The Venona decrypts identified numerous Soviet agents operating in the United States and Britain during and after World War II, including Klaus Fuchs, the Rosenbergs, and others. Declassified and released publicly beginning in 1995.

Vichy France — The French government established following France's defeat by Germany in June 1940, based in the spa town of Vichy and governing the unoccupied southern zone of France under the leadership of Marshal Philippe Pétain. The Vichy government collaborated with the German occupation in numerous respects, including implementing anti-Jewish legislation and cooperating with German intelligence operations. Ended with the Allied liberation of France in 1944.

W

Welrod — A suppressed bolt-action pistol developed at SOE's Station IX for use in close-range assassination and elimination operations. Its report was approximately equivalent to a handclap, making it suitable for indoor use without alerting nearby personnel. Issued to SOE agents and resistance fighters across occupied Europe and Southeast Asia, and remained in production in various classified contexts for decades after the war.

Wireless operator — An agent trained to operate a clandestine radio set for communication between a field network and its headquarters. Among the most dangerous roles in any resistance or intelligence network, as radio transmissions could be located by direction-finding equipment. The average life expectancy of an SOE wireless operator in France in 1943 was approximately six weeks.

World War I (The Great War) — The global conflict of 1914 to 1918, fought primarily in Europe between the Allied Powers (Britain, France, Russia, and later the United States) and the Central Powers (Germany, Austria-Hungary, and the Ottoman Empire). The first industrialized war on a global scale, and the conflict in which modern military intelligence, including systematic use of female agents, was first extensively developed.

World War II (The Second World War) — The global conflict of 1939 to 1945, fought between the Allied powers (Britain, the Soviet Union, the United States, and others) and the

Axis powers (Germany, Italy, and Japan). The largest and deadliest conflict in human history, and the period in which modern intelligence operations — including the systematic use of agents, sabotage networks, deception operations, and signals intelligence — reached their full development.

A Note On Sources

Shadow Armies is a work of narrative nonfiction. Every person, event, operation, and organization described in this book is real. No characters have been invented, no dialogue fabricated, and no events dramatized beyond what the historical record supports. Where the historical record is contested, uncertain, or incomplete, those limitations are acknowledged directly in the text.

The primary sources for this book draw on declassified intelligence records from the British National Archives at Kew, the Polish Institute and Sikorski Museum in London, and the United States National Archives at College Park, Maryland. These collections contain SOE operational records, OSS mission reports, AK command documents, and postwar debriefs that form the documentary foundation of the operations described here.

The author has also drawn extensively on the published historical scholarship listed in the bibliography that follows, as well as on firsthand accounts written by participants including Nancy Wake, Fitzroy Maclean, R.V. Jones, Basil Davidson, Jan Karski, and Vladimir Dedijer. Where firsthand accounts conflict with the documentary record or with each other, the text acknowledges the discrepancy rather than arbitrating it artificially.

Readers who wish to pursue any of the operations, individuals, or organizations described in this book will find the bibliography a reliable starting point for further research.

Bibliography

General Works on the Second World War

Beevor, Antony. *D-Day: The Battle for Normandy.* Viking, 2009.

Beevor, Antony. *The Second World War.* Little, Brown, 2012.

Keegan, John. *The Second World War.* Viking, 1989.

Ziemke, Earl F. *Stalingrad to Berlin: The German Defeat in the East.* Office of the Chief of Military History, 1968.

France and the French Resistance

Buckmaster, Maurice. *Specially Employed: The Story of British Aid to French Patriots of the Resistance.* Batchworth Press, 1952.

Foot, M.R.D. *SOE in France: An Account of the Work of the British Special Operations Executive in France 1940–1944.* HMSO, 1966.

Hastings, Max. *Das Reich: The March of the 2nd SS Panzer Division Through France.* Michael Joseph, 1981.

Helm, Sarah. *A Life in Secrets: Vera Atkins and the Lost Agents of SOE.* Little, Brown, 2005.

Macksey, Kenneth. *The Partisans of Europe in the Second World War*. Hart-Davis MacGibbon, 1975.

Marshall, Robert. *All the King's Men: The Truth Behind SOE's Greatest Wartime Disaster*. Collins, 1988.

Moorehead, Caroline. *Village of Secrets: Defying the Nazis in Vichy France*. Chatto & Windus, 2014.

Ousby, Ian. *Occupation: The Ordeal of France 1940–1944*. John Murray, 1997.

Pearson, Michael. *The Cruel Trap*. Macmillan, 1978.

Vinen, Richard. *The Unfree French: Life Under the Occupation*. Allen Lane, 2006.

Wake, Nancy. *The White Mouse*. Macmillan Australia, 1985.

SOE and Special Operations

Binney, Marcus. *The Women Who Lived for Danger: The Agents of the Special Operations Executive*. Hodder & Stoughton, 2002.

Irwin, Will. *The Jedburghs: The Secret History of the Allied Special Forces, France 1944*. PublicAffairs, 2005.

Escott, Beryl E. *Mission Improbable: A Salute to the RAF Women of SOE in Wartime France*. Patrick Stephens, 1991.

Ford, Roger. *Steel from the Sky: The Jedburgh Raiders, France 1944*. Weidenfeld & Nicolson, 2004.

Stafford, David. *Britain and European Resistance 1940–1945: A Survey of the Special Operations Executive*. Macmillan, 1980.

Poland and the Polish Underground

Garliński, Józef. *Hitler's Last Weapons: The Underground War Against the V1 and V2*. Julian Friedmann, 1978.

Karski, Jan. *Story of a Secret State: My Report to the World*. Houghton Mifflin, 1944.

Korboński, Stefan. *The Polish Underground State: A Guide to the Underground 1939–1945*. East European Quarterly, 1978.

Nowak, Jan. *Courier from Warsaw*. Wayne State University Press, 1982.

Pilecki, Witold. *The Auschwitz Volunteer: Beyond Bravery*. Translated by Jarek Garliński. Aquila Polonica, 2012.

Tucholski, Jędrzej. *Cichociemni*. Instytut Wydawniczy PAX, 1984.

Wood, E. Thomas, and Stanisław M. Jankowski. *Karski: How One Man Tried to Stop the Holocaust*. John Wiley & Sons, 1994.

V-Weapons and Scientific Intelligence

Irving, David. *The Mare's Nest: The German Secret Weapons Campaign and Allied Countermeasures*. William Kimber, 1964.

Jones, R.V. *Most Secret War: British Scientific Intelligence 1939–1945*. Hamish Hamilton, 1978.

Babington Smith, Constance. *Evidence in Camera: The Story of Photographic Intelligence in World War II*. Chatto & Windus, 1958.

Yugoslavia and the Partisan Resistance

Davidson, Basil. *Special Operations Europe: Scenes from the Anti-Nazi War*. Victor Gollancz, 1980.

Dedijer, Vladimir. *Tito*. Simon & Schuster, 1953.

Dedijer, Vladimir. *The War Diaries of Vladimir Dedijer*. University of Michigan Press, 1990.

Đilas, Milovan. *Conversations with Stalin.* Rupert Hart-Davis, 1962.

Maclean, Fitzroy. *Eastern Approaches.* Jonathan Cape, 1949.

Martin, David. *The Web of Disinformation: Churchill's Yugoslav Blunder.* Harcourt Brace Jovanovich, 1990.

Ridley, Jasper. *Tito: A Biography.* Constable, 1994.

Tomasevich, Jozo. *War and Revolution in Yugoslavia 1941–1945: The Chetniks.* Stanford University Press, 1975.

Firsthand Accounts and Memoirs

Braddon, Russell. *Nancy Wake: The Story of a Very Brave Woman.* Cassell, 1956.

Fuller, Jean Overton. *Double Webs: Light on the Secret Agents' War in France.* Putnam, 1958.

Maclean, Fitzroy. *Eastern Approaches.* Jonathan Cape, 1949.

Recommended Further Reading

For readers wishing to explore the broader history of resistance warfare and special operations in the Second World War, the following works are particularly recommended:

Atkinson, Rick. *An Army at Dawn: The War in North Africa, 1942–1943.* Henry Holt, 2002.

Hastings, Max. *The Secret War: Spies, Codes and Guerrillas 1939–1945.* William Collins, 2015.

Larson, Erik. *The Splendid and the Vile: A Saga of Churchill, Family, and Defiance During the Blitz.* Crown, 2020.

Macintyre, Ben. *Double Cross: The True Story of the D-Day Spies.* Crown, 2012.

Macintyre, Ben. *SAS: Rogue Heroes — The Authorized Wartime History*. Crown, 2016.

Olson, Lynne. *Madame Fourcade's Secret War: The Daring Young Woman Who Led France's Largest Spy Network Against Hitler*. Random House, 2019.

Acknowledgements

A book about people who risked everything in the service of others cannot be written without acknowledging the debt owed to the historians, archivists, and researchers whose work made this one possible.

The scholarship of M.R.D. Foot, Jozo Tomasevich, R.V. Jones, and Józef Garliński forms the documentary backbone of this book. Their decades of painstaking research into the records of SOE, the Armia Krajowa, the Yugoslav Partisans, and the V-weapons program established the factual foundation on which narrative accounts like this one depend. Any errors of fact or interpretation in these pages are mine alone.

The staffs of the Polish Institute and Sikorski Museum in London, the National Archives at Kew, and the Imperial War Museum deserve recognition for preserving and making accessible the primary source materials without which the history of resistance warfare could not be written.

This book is published under the Crazy Dog Publishing imprint, and would not exist without the support of everyone who has encouraged the Shadow Wars Series from its earliest stages.

Finally — and most importantly — this book exists because the people whose stories it tells chose to fight when fighting was the most dangerous thing they could do. The least that can be offered in return is that their stories be told as accurately and as honestly as the historical record allows.

Chuck Watson

Crazy Dog Publishing

Also by Chuck Watson

Traitors, Spies, and Secret Agents: True Stories of the Men and Women Who Fought America's Secret Civil War

The Shadow Wars Series • Book Two

While armies clashed at Gettysburg and Vicksburg, a parallel war was being fought in cipher rooms and prison tunnels by men and women whose greatest weapon was the ability to disappear into plain sight. Twenty true stories from the shadow war that ran alongside America's bloodiest conflict.

Blown Cover: True Stories of Cold War Spies, Double Agents, and Deadly Betrayals

The Shadow Wars Series • Book Three

In the corridors of power in Washington and Moscow, the most dangerous war in history was fought without armies. Twenty true stories of the spies, double agents, and defectors whose betrayals brought the world to the edge of annihilation more than once.

The Invisible Arsenal: True Stories of the Bombmakers, Forgers, and Craftsmen Who Armed History's Most Dangerous Spies

The Shadow Wars Series • Book Four

History remembers the spies. It forgets the people who made them possible. Twenty true stories of the chemists, engineers, tailors, and forgers who worked in secret government workshops to build the tools of covert war — and whose names never made it into the file.

———◦———

Dangerous by Design: True Stories of Women Who Lived Double Lives During the Most Dangerous Conflicts in History

The Shadow Wars Series • Book Five

They were recruited because their handlers believed women were invisible in wartime. That assumption was the greatest miscalculation the intelligence services of two world wars ever made. Twenty true stories of the women who lived double lives across WWI, WWII, and the Cold War — and changed the outcome of wars that history assigned to men.

———◦———

The L.A.U.G.H. Method

A laugh-out-loud guide for everyday adults who feel like they're barely holding it together. Equal parts humor and heart, this book reminds readers that it's okay to be imperfect, overwhelmed, and still doing just fine.

About the Author

Chuck Watson is a writer, woodworker, and lifelong storyteller based in Minnesota. Through his independent publishing imprint, Crazy Dog Publishing, he writes across multiple genres — always with an eye for the stories that deserve to be told and the readers who deserve to enjoy them.

He is the author of *The L.A.U.G.H. Method*, a humor and self-help book that blends laugh-out-loud wit with genuine grace for everyday adults navigating life's messier moments. *Shadow Armies* is his first work of narrative nonfiction and the opening volume of the Shadow Wars Series — an ongoing exploration of the secret fighters, covert operations, and shadow wars that shaped the course of history.

When he isn't writing, Chuck can be found putzing around in his workshop.

DID YOU ENJOY THIS BOOK?

If *Shadow Armies* stuck with you — if it made you see World War II a little differently — I'd appreciate it if you took a moment to leave a review on your favorite book site or retailer.

That's how books like this get found. And how the people in these pages don't get forgotten.

Thanks for reading.

— Chuck Watson

Connect with Chuck:

Website: chuckwatsonauthor.com

Email: hello@chuckwatsonauthor.com

Facebook: facebook.com/chuckwatsonauthor

Instagram: @chuckwatsonauthor

TikTok: @chuckwatsonauthor